TRUE
TO THE
LINE

TRUE
TO THE
LINE
A Hunting Life

Adrian Dangar

Quiller

*This book is dedicated
to the memory of Tristan Voorspuy.
He gave me a life after hunting.*

Copyright ©2017 Adrian Dangar

First published in the UK in 2017 by
Quiller, an imprint of Quiller Publishing Ltd

Reprinted in 2018

British Library Cataloguing-in-Publication Data
A catalogue record for this book is available from
the British Library

ISBN 978 1 84689 359 9

Edited by Paul Middleton
Jacket designed by Arabella Ainslie
Book designed by Guy Callaby
Printed and bound in Great Britain by TJ Books Ltd, Cornwall

Quiller

An imprint of Quiller Publishing Ltd
Wykey House, Wykey, Shrewsbury SY4 1JA
Tel: 01939 261616
Email: info@quillerbooks.com
Website: www.quillerpublishing.com

Contents

Acknowledgements

There are many people to thank for their help not only with this book, but also during my time as an MFH. My parents sit at the top of that list for instilling in me a passion for the chase and encouraging me to pursue my dream of hunting hounds. Sidney Bailey and Martin Scott for so happily taking me under their wings with the VWH, and all those kind people who lent me horses to hunt during my Cirencester days. Captain Ian Farquhar for his unconditional support throughout my time as an MFH, and for kindly writing the foreword to this book. The late James Daly for the gift of Ledbury Celebrate '84, and in Bright Beacon, my first point-to-point winner. Tim Millar for taking me on as his joint master when I was 24 years old, and the late Dermot Kelly for the gift of his red coat, and the opportunity to steward at Peterborough Royal Foxhound Show. All those who provided hospitality and support on Dartmoor when I needed it most, particularly the late Charles Doughty, Sue Sprott, Carrie and Charlie Lawson, the entire Cole family and the late Mike Howard, with special thanks to the saintly Wendy Doidge for doing my washing for three long years.

The Countess of Feversham, Major John Shaw and Hugh Murray Wells – all sadly no longer with us – for their exceptional kindness and encouragement to a young amateur huntsman in North Yorkshire, and James and Mary Holt for their constant support, generosity and hospitality at Ravenswick. Ginny Johnson and the late Joan Crosfield for permanently open houses in Leicestershire during my time at the Quorn, and to John Mills, Gary Cracknell and others who gave so generously of their time to help with the difficult job of stewarding. I owe a debt of thanks to all my patient and supportive joint masters including Andrew Osborne for two seasons at the Sinnington, and Richard Carden, Charles Geary,

Joss Hanbury and Rad Thomas for the duration of my short time in Leicestershire. The difficult job of organising a hunting country is made so much easier and more enjoyable by good hunt staff and I would like to thank all who helped me along the way, amateur and professional alike, but most notably Richard Mould, Neil Brooksbank and Caroline Scott, respectively the best kennel huntsman, terrierman and stud groom I could ever hope for.

Not forgetting everyone who has welcomed hounds and horses over their land wherever I have carried the horn, and those gamekeepers who left me a fox or two to hunt, offered valuable advice, and made generous compromises to their own sport. I will never forget the hounds, horses and terriers with which I have shared my life, and wish there were some way of rewarding them in the afterlife for their bravery and devotion to duty. The late Tristan Voorspuy, who in helping to establish Wild and Exotic gave me a life after hunting, and those kind editors who have commissioned my features for, amongst others, *Country Life*, *The Field*, *Horse & Hound* and *Trout & Salmon*.

I would like to thank my father, Catherine Austen and Marcus Armytage for proof reading the manuscript of this book, and the artist and MFH, Daniel Crane, for his charming sketches. Thanks also to all those who have generously given permission for their photographs or paintings to be used without charge, including Jim Meads, Ray Paulson, Mark Egerton and Heather Tylor. Special thanks to Andrew and Gilly Johnston and all the excellent team at Quiller Publishing for guiding me through the complexities of writing my first book. Finally, thanks to my wife, Rachel, a quite exceptional lady who came late into my life but has enriched it ever since with her grace, beauty, wisdom and kindness.

Foreword

I first met Adrian Dangar when he came to Twyford Mill, our then home in the Bicester country as a whipper-in – later huntsman to the Stowe Beagles. It soon became apparent that not only had he inherited his parents' love of the chase but also their charm. It was not long before Mrs Farquhar gave him a day on a new small hunter she had just purchased – an honour indeed!

He rode it rather well and was profuse with his thanks and was considered a good egg all round.

We got to know Adrian better when his great friend and co-conspirator at Stowe, Frank Houghton-Brown, became our terrierman, so when the Spooners and West Dartmoor asked me if I knew of a dedicated and tough young man who might fulfil the role of master and huntsman in that demanding country, Adrian came immediately to mind. He accepted – was a round peg in a round hole and, as they say, the rest is history.

The Spooners was followed by the Sinnington, a spell at the Quorn and thence back to the Sinnington. During these thirty-odd years he made a name for himself as a fine huntsman but also as an imaginative hound breeder. He has left behind him a legacy, especially in the Sinnington, of hounds that not only perform well in the field but also came up to the mark on the flags. This all while he was also helping with important work in the political field, especially with the shooting fraternity and at the same time having fun pursuing all manner of quarry around the world!

Reading his book also brings to light two other qualities that are important in the modern day master: an inherent gift to get on with your fellow human beings and an ability to organise.

He enjoyed the company of his landowners and farmers and they enjoyed his. They were both able to see the funny side when things went wrong, which sometimes they invariably do. He was meticulous in writing up his diaries, a discipline that is easy to forego in a hectic workload.

On a personal note, over the years I have greatly enjoyed Adrian's company and can recommend this book to any true-blooded sportsman for its depth of knowledge and humour.

A good read.

Captain Ian Farquhar, LVO, MFH

The Happiest Man in England

The happiest man in England rose an hour before the dawn;
The stars were in the purple and the dew was on the lawn;
He hurried to the stable through the dim light of the stars,
And there his good horse waited, clicking rings and bridle-bars.
The happiest man in England took a grey lock in his hand
And settled in his saddle like a seagull on the sand.
Then from the shadowy kennel all the eager pack outpoured,
And the happiest man in England saw them scatter on the sward.
And where the blind ditch narrows and the deep-set gorse begins
He waved his pack to covert, and he cheered them through the whins.
He heard old Gladstone whimper, then Merryman give tongue;
He saw the green gorse shaking as the whole pack checked and swung;
Then through the ditch came creeping a shy cub lithe and lean,
And nothing but a cocked grey ear betrayed that he was seen.
The happiest man in England blew the freedom of the pass,
And two-and-twenty couple backed his music on the grass.
He holds no brief for slaughter, but the cubs must take their chance;
The weak must first go under that the strong may lead the dance;
And when the grey strides out and shakes the foam- flecks from his rings
The happiest man in England would not change his place with kings

Taken from the poem by William Henry Ogilvie (1869–1963)

CHAPTER 1

Earliest days

I woke very early on the morning of 1 May 1987 to the sound of hounds singing from their lodges less than two hundred yards from my bedroom, and life felt good. Not just good, almost perfect in fact, for this was a moment that I had been working towards all of my short life. At twenty-four years old I had become the master and huntsman to a pack of foxhounds, and my new charges were summoning me from my bed. No one has ever got changed quicker than I did that morning, nor sprinted faster up the narrow concrete path that leads from the white huntsman's house to the Spooners and West Dartmoor kennels perched on the very edge of the last great wilderness of southern England. I may not have realised it at the time, but I was now set firmly on a path that I would follow through its twists and turns, highs and lows, for the next thirty-odd years.

I could not possibly have walked into the kennels that glorious May morning and assumed sole charge of a pack of foxhounds without having already devoted an inordinate amount of time to hunting in all its guises, nor could I have garnered the confidence and knowledge to do so were it not for the help, guidance and support of so many from my formative years. My parents first instilled in me a love and respect for the chase that has endured to this day. They hunted hard with the Beaufort and Avon Vale, walked a succession of hound puppies and went like smoke across country on horses they had made themselves.

My mother once got into trouble with the late 10th Duke of Beaufort, who saw fit to send her home after the temptation of jumping an inviting hedge beside an open gate was just too great to resist, although he later wrote her the most charming letter of apology. It would not be an exaggeration to claim that hunting was a religion of sorts in our household, with masters of hounds being akin to the saints, if not God himself; a belief and acceptance that the MFH was beyond reproach was fundamental, and it was rare for either of my parents to utter a word of criticism against those who provided their sport. I am told I attended a meet of the York & Ainsty (South) in a pram at my grandparents' home, Melbourne Hall in Yorkshire, when just a few months old, but it is entirely appropriate that my earliest memory is of a whippet called Chico and a broken-coated terrier named Badger working together to catch a rat in a pigsty. I can still see the quarry running in that strange shuffling gait along the top of a wall, and Chico's jaws opening to snatch it from safety.

Dispatch to a cold and positively Dickensian boarding school in Berkshire soon afterwards was not a decision I thought to question at the time, but perhaps living in a dormitory where it was so cold at night that urine in pots underneath boys' beds froze solid was preparation for long, cold days in the saddle in later life. During my time at Lambrook I busied myself breeding mice, catching grass snakes and spearing gudgeon in the Lamb Brook with a sewing needle lashed to a bamboo cane. Another favourite pastime was shaking milk that had been poured into an empty mustard pot in order to make butter, for the tiny morsel of yellow gold cut into the shape of a flower that accompanied each meal was never sufficient for a permanently hungry schoolboy.

A disused railway line that serves as the boundary between the Beaufort and Avon Vale Hunts divided the Wiltshire fields we owned at Stanley Mill, and during long summer holidays offered a playground in which to pursue rabbits with a bobbery pack of terriers, lurchers and whippets. I can still smell the acrid whiff of a freshly killed rabbit, feel the briar scratches on tender arms and taste the honeyed draft of cider proffered by a neighbouring farmer after one particularly memorable evening's sport. The River Marden chugged slowly along the northern boundary of our small farm, gurgling into a deep still pool beneath a ruined aqueduct my brother and I were forbidden to cross. No trout swam through these quiet waters, but roach, chub and dace flourished and enticed in equal measure. Not being anglers, my parents did not think to point out that tying a hook to an ancient greased line from the attic was never going to catch me a fish. Eventually I discovered monofilament line, and with the guidance of a Ladybird book on fishing taught myself how to tie a blood knot and secure the hook. I caught a fat silver roach that day, stabbed it thoroughly with my sheath knife and ran home in triumph to the kitchen.

However, rabbiting, fishing and other boyish pursuits were no substitute for hunting, which already had me in its thrall, and holidays between September and April were devoted to riding behind the Avon Vale or Duke of Beaufort's hounds. My conveyance was a mealy-mouthed bay Exmoor pony named Flashman, who was not above bucking me off when spring hunting in the hills above Bath but was an otherwise perfect conveyance for a child more interested in venery that riding. Flashman was replaced by the racier Llewellyn, a talented grey on whom I enjoyed my first red-letter day across the Bushton Vale behind a straight-necked fox found in Hangings covert above Clyffe Pypard.

Major Gerald Gundry was hunting the Beaufort doghounds that Thursday, which combined fleeting glimpses of his pack driving on across an unkempt and woolly landscape interspersed with fences looming thick and fast to both challenge and conquer. I lost a stirrup leather amongst the mud, bustle and gallop of the hunt, only to be rescued by kindness in the shape of Hugh Dalgety, who wasted no time in fashioning a substitute from bailer twine. The fox was run to ground after a five-mile point and from that day on I relished the ride, and began to appreciate the complexities of venery, bravery and horsemanship that combine to offer the complete hunting experience.

Brian Gupwell hunted the Beaufort bitches in those days, a supremely elegant and beautifully turned-out professional who presented me with the brush of a cub killed in Ashpole after a busy September morning when I was ten years old, but I had to wait another whole year before being blooded by the legendary Sidney Bailey in his second season as huntsman to the VWH. The occasion was an invitation meet of the Gloucestershire pack at Imber, an isolated and deserted village at the heart of Salisbury Plain in South and West Wilts country. During an extraordinary spring day the field were treated to spectacular views of hounds hunting across open country, including the sight of a fox getting to ground just feet in front of the leading hounds. The pad of a less fortunate one hangs in my office to this day. My first experience of hunting across open country made a lasting impression, and helped cultivate a love of hunting in the type of wild hill country that was soon to become my new home.

CHAPTER 2

Yorkshire

I cannot pretend I was enthusiastic about moving north to Yorkshire, for my feet and mind had become firmly planted in the Wiltshire meadows surrounding Stanley Mill, but one has little say in such matters when only twelve years old. Our new house lay at the end of a mile-long drive, overlooked steep fields rising to the heathery horizon of Eskdaleside and was bounded on the south by the beguiling River Esk, home to wild brown trout, salmon, sea trout and vast numbers of eels that attacked worms offered by my brother and me with gusto. Below the house there was a ford across a shallow stretch of the river that led steeply uphill to our nearest neighbours, Derek and Linda Gardiner and the Goathland foxhounds, which could be heard singing joyously at night. I soon realised that my new surroundings were something rather special.

Apart from the estates of Mulgrave and Egton, little shooting took place in the Goathland country in those days but for whatever reason foxes were less numerous than I had been used to, although it occasionally all came together to produce wonderful sport. Apart from jumping on and off the single-track railway line during a particularly fine hunt, and another occasion when the train stopped to give someone who had fallen off their horse a lift, my memories are of hounds, terriers and foxes: Granite '73 single-handedly dispatching a fox in the Coombes high above the Murk Esk, hounds pulling another one down on Sleights moor, and my black-and-tan terrier, Boozer, bolting a fox one September morning from Gatehouse Rocks close to the village that lends the hunt its name. By then Jamie Cameron had arrived to take on the mastership as a young amateur, and taught me that it is better to eat at someone else's table as a bachelor huntsman than cook for oneself at home. Jamie became such a frequent visitor to our house that a room was earmarked for his exclusive use. Somewhere I still have the handwritten note he presented me with after the morning from Gatehouse Rocks: *This is to certify that Boozer is a game terrier to fox.*

Whether hunting rabbits to ground for the attention of my ferret, Jaybird, raking around Eskdale after the occasional and elusive pheasant, bolting foxes for the Goathland or hunting moorhens and rats in summer, Boozer was my constant companion during school holidays. One January afternoon hounds ran a fox into the rocks at Glaisdale Head, which lies at the top end of a picture-perfect dale surrounded on three sides by wild moorland. The rocky fissures reach deep into the very bowels of the earth, which is perhaps why I was allowed to try my dog ahead of those belonging to the regular terriermen, Paul Marsay and Bryan Kidd. We listened to Boozer's baying fading as he crept ever deeper into the side of the hill until nothing more could be heard save for impatient and intermittent cries from the waiting pack. Eventually darkness came down and there was nothing for it but to temporarily abandon the terrier, but not before leaving my crumpled Barbour coat outside the entrance to the earth. My father and I returned much later beneath silvery moonlight to find Boozer curled up asleep on the coat, his hair glistening with hoar frost that had lacquered the dale an eerie shade of pale. It is not known what became of the fox.

Other excitements waited on the southern side of the North York Moors, where grander packs hunted the hills and vale that rolled out towards the distant city of York. The closest of these was the Sinnington, where Willy Poole and his Welsh outcrosses provided fine sport in a well-foxed country that could have been fashioned with hunting in mind. I enjoyed the second five-mile point of my life behind those hounds, and marvelled at how they went like smoke from Ness Kelds deep into the Castle Howard estate. Christmas Eves were spent hunting with the Middleton from Westow, where Boozer's breeder and close family friend, Colonel Nick Crossley, shared the horn with Dennis Sturgeon, a kind and widely respected professional who invited me into the kennels at Birdsall to see hounds being fed after hunting.

CHAPTER 3

Stowe

My next stroke of great good fortune was to be sent to boarding school at Stowe shortly after our new home in Yorkshire had been established. Famously described by the first headmaster, J. F. Roxburgh, as being a place that would inspire students to 'recognise beauty whenever they see it for the rest of their lives', the school's sprawling grounds extended to seven hundred acres of Buckinghamshire countryside dotted with exquisite temples in varying stages of decay and three substantial lakes. We kept ferrets in a corrugated shed handily positioned between the main school building and the classrooms, which allowed them to be fed and mucked out on the way to lessons each morning. That ferrets were permitted to live in such a prime location was not questioned; perhaps it had something to do with the tall beech hedge that concealed their home from several hundred students who passed within feet of it every day. But best of all Stowe had – and has to this day – a fine pack of beagles, which are kennelled at the Boycott Pavilions a hundred yards from the main drive, their diet supplemented by dustbin loads of school food disdained by students on a daily basis.

Although I managed to survive the full course at Stowe, things got off to a shaky start when as new boys we were given two weeks' immunity from punishment in order to learn the school rules. It seems I was the only boy who took this concession literally by spending ten memorable days doing little else but exploring the grounds, fishing and beagling. My honeymoon came to an abrupt end when I was summoned into my housemaster's study and soundly thrashed, but the real lesson learnt was that authority in all its many guises could never be completely trusted. After that, I started attending lessons, but the highlights of my week were Tuesdays and Saturdays when the Stowe beagles met at farms, villages and pubs within a 20-mile radius of the school.

Being kennel huntsman to an amateur is a difficult position at any time, and one that is best suited to men of certain temperament and character, but to discharge this delicate role when the masters and huntsman are schoolboys must be extraordinarily challenging. Stowe was fortunate to have procured the services of former factory worker and countryman, John Thornton, who was known to all as Nat, although we boys occasionally referred to him as Pinhead behind his back. Nat was a brilliant and long-suffering man who understood exactly the right balance between allowing his young masters leeway and intervening in time to avert disaster both on and off the hunting field. That he was already grooming his charges for future glory as masters of foxhounds was lost on us at the time, but I have never forgotten much of his sound advice. We were cautioned against owning a flash car, which would risk a reduction in the master's guarantee, and to marry for love but crucially, 'love where money is'. As it turned out, many of the MFHs spawned by Stowe since then chose to heed the former piece of advice but to ignore the latter.

By the time I arrived in 1976, Nat had established himself as a worthy successor to the hunt's first KH, John Atkinson, by maintaining a lovely level pack that hunted as well as they looked. Boys interested in beagling were encouraged to help down at the kennels as much as possible, which would in turn be rewarded by an invitation to whip in, wearing the hunt's green coat with a dark-blue collar. Having served my time whipping-in to Paul Burditt and James Fanshawe, who now trains racehorses at Newmarket, it was my turn to carry the horn during the 1980–81 season, although I had managed to catch a hare in unusual circumstances the previous year.

We had been entertained by Captain Brian Bell at Todenham Manor, which is some way from the Stowe's own territory, and enjoyed a busy day in the cream of the Warwickshire Hunt country. At the end of the day we were several hounds light, so I was delegated to take the main body of the pack home whilst the others helped James Fanshawe recover the missing hounds. I was leading hounds up a narrow lane in fading light when I bumped into our host in a state of some considerable excitement. Captain Bell told me that his spaniel had picked up and dropped a very tired hare just a few minutes earlier in a large clump of nettles. He cast his eyes over the pack at my heels and suggested I run them through the undergrowth, 'just to be sure'. When the nettle patch was blank it seemed obvious to hold hounds down the adjacent hedgerow, which resulted in them marking furiously at a large rabbit hole. The hare was only 18 inches in and, having broken her neck the same way as I dispatched rabbits in purse nets, the beagles had their reward and I became for a short while afterwards the most insufferable schoolboy in Britain.

The following September my season as huntsman kicked off as usual with a trip north to hunt the rolling Northumbrian countryside either side of Hadrian's Wall. The Northumberland Beagling Festival was the brainchild of the late Colonel Leonard Gibson, whose Newcastle and District beagles showed superlative sport in a country large and wild enough to accommodate many less-fortunate packs during a three-week jamboree that the Stowe were privileged to be part of, if only for a few precious days. I may have killed my first hare in dubious circumstances the previous season, but there was nothing controversial about the next one following the meet at Bradley after a fine ninety-minute hunt. Our quarry was reported as very tired moments before hounds streamed over a 5ft-high wall to claim their reward in a sieve bed, which she had crept into via a tiny gap in the stones.

I remember equally well, but for very different reasons, a second epic hunt that had to be abandoned in the interests of pacifying an irate farmer whose bullocks had seen quite enough of hounds for the day, if not the season. As I led hounds away from the scene I spotted our beaten hare crouching amongst thistles just yards away. The temptation was almost too great to resist, and I am afraid that I protested Nat's instructions most bitterly that evening. 'David', he said, referring to a recent past master of the beagles, 'would not have thought twice about getting hounds out of there'. I went to bed seething with angst, and decided that I could never be a David of the hunting world. As it turned out, nor could he, for his name has never cropped up in hunting circles since.

We had many fine hunts that season, each one meticulously recorded for posterity in the school hunting diary that is passed down through successive generations of schoolboy huntsmen. By the end of season I had learnt an enormous amount from that fabulous little pack, which consistently accounted for their quarry after long hunts with a style and frequency that I have seldom seen emulated. Names such as Tingewick, Water Stratford, Dadford, Radclive, Marsh Gibbon, Preston Capes, Weston and Everdon resonate with blurred memories of fine hunts and the unique camaraderie of a schoolboy pack. I can close my eyes and see hounds such as Rockwood, Roxburgh, Starlight and Willow as if they were still frolicking on exercise beneath the long, green avenue of trees leading up to the main school. Frank Houghton-Brown and Tom Bannister, were my principal whipper-ins, the latter tragically killed many years later whilst in office as a joint master of the Pendle Forest and Craven Harriers.

If Tuesdays and Saturdays were devoted to hare hunting, Sundays during winter were sacrosanct for the equally enthusiastic pursuit of rabbits with ferrets and purse nets. The normal procedure was to rise very early, grab some breakfast with the domestic staff and head off on bicycles at chilly first light. Two or three ferrets were carried in a .303 ammo box pilfered from the CCF stores and threaded along the handlebars so that it was possible to avoid collision with the box by pedalling with one knee held at right angles; nets and game bags were slung over shoulders. We did not bother to take any sustenance on these expeditions; such luxuries would have to wait until return at nightfall. Although ferreting was not encouraged by the school, it was certainly accepted, however, the issue of cutting Sunday chapel became increasingly problematic and ultimately led to a ban on ferrets being kept within the grounds. The resulting dilemma was resolved when Mr Jenkins, whose daughter, Bronwen, was in my academic year, accommodated them in his farmyard at Dadford less than half a mile from their former home. The headmaster smiled and turned the other way, whilst his secretary and my house matron continued to purchase for £1.50, a brace of fresh, gutted rabbits every Monday morning throughout winter during the rest of my time at Stowe.

The unwritten rule was that any boy wishing to inherit the mantle of chief ferreter should serve his apprenticeship with the current incumbent, and it was with this in mind that I wandered into the Temple houseroom for junior boys one January afternoon and asked a young Frank Houghton-Brown if he would be interested in helping out the following day. It snowed hard that night, but we reached Sir Thomas Wilson's farm at Lillingstone Dayrell without too many hiccups and at once set to work. Frank distinguished himself by catching with his bare hands a rabbit that had bolted from a hole concealed by snow; his quarry may have been slowed up a little by the white stuff but no one had ever managed that before. On the way home Frank's decrepit bike gave up the ghost and there was nothing for it but to take on board the rabbits he had been carrying and abandon him to his fate. Having battled through snowdrifts on the Roman road I eventually arrived home to find Frank smug, warm and changed having been rescued, bathed, fed and returned by a kind lady driver. After that Frank started to help out with the ferreting on a regular basis.

Other delights at Stowe included the Oxford Water Lake, which every visitor to the school must cross via a beautiful stone bridge that dates from 1761. The waters beneath were just fresh enough to sustain a population of rainbow trout stocked for the benefit of a students' fly-fishing club, although hungry schoolboys found sticking to the one-brace-a-week limit somewhat challenging. This infuriated George Monbiot, another keen fisherman, fellow student and self-appointed water bailiff, who made it his mission to catch the transgressors. Despite creeping down to the Oxford Water at random first light throughout summer George never succeeded in apprehending a poacher. If he had chosen not to approach through a field of sentinel sheep he might have had better luck, although on one infamous occasion the miscreants fled leaving behind a large haul of trout on the bank. It was inevitable that I would cross swords with the future *Guardian* columnist, although I had to feel sorry for Monbiot when drawing a swim in the school fishing competition that he had been ground baiting for weeks. I caught an enormous tench that won the competition, infuriated my rival, and earned me the most dubious award of house colours in the history of Temple House.

Towards the end of my time at Stowe, spring holidays were given over to hunting with the fell packs of the Cumbrian Lake District, where Johnny Richardson was carrying the horn in the twilight years of a long and distinguished career with the Blencathra Hunt. The most entertaining sport followed dawn lambing calls when just a few couple of old and reliable hounds were taken out for the specific purpose of bringing a lamb-killing fox to justice. As our base was a B&B at Threlkeld, where the Blencathra hounds are kennelled, it made sense to jump in with them when the hunt van passed our door long before dawn, which would have scarcely broken when the small pack was taken amongst the ewes and lambs grazing the in-bye land of the valley floor. Sterns lashing in the half-light, hounds would normally strike up within minutes and pick away at the line until reaching the open fell where the pace often increased on clean ground. Sometimes the fox was unkennelled and run down on the hill; often he was marked in a big borran of rocks, which called for terriers and spades to complete the job. Thanks to the Hunting Act and thermal imaging, this most justifiable, selective and purest form of hunting with hounds has now been replaced by the high-powered rifle.

A chance encounter with Charlie Ripman on the fells one March resulted in an invitation to visit Exmoor the following week, and establish another fixture in the sporting calendar that was to endure for several happy springs. Charlie, who was reporting for the *Shooting Times* magazine, assured Frank and me that his mother would simply love to see us at her White Horse Hotel in Exford, which is the very epicentre of West Country hunting and home to the Devon and Somerset staghounds. The deal he brokered was free board and lodging at her Duredon Farm in exchange for some log chopping and bartending at night, but with Exmoor Hunt lambing calls, foxhunting with several packs and spring staghunting to choose from most days, there was little time for any domestic chores. Sally, whose other son, Martyn Lee, was hunting the Taunton Vale, chuckled generously in that rich voice of hers and declined to enforce her side of the bargain. To follow hounds across Exmoor on a horse was way beyond budget, but by running, walking and driving it was possible to enjoy some wonderful sport and absorb the new-found venery of staghunting.

Back at Stowe I busied myself with Chaucer, Milton and Shakespeare and defied my tutors' dire predictions by gaining A level grades that were more than adequate for the Royal Agriculture College at Cirencester. I left clutching a copy of my *Cantata Stoica*, in which a contemporary described our seat of learning as 'Stowe Country Club for Boys'. My headmaster, Christopher Turner, had once written to my parents to prevail on them to remind me that I was in receipt of two generous concessions at Stowe. The first was being allowed to keep ferrets and run what he described as a thriving business selling rabbits, the second being granted the time to go beagling twice weekly against a backdrop of failing academic studies. Rather to my surprise he described me in my final report as being the school's patron saint of ferreting, and to my even greater astonishment wrote that 'one cannot help liking him in spite of everything'. With these compliments ringing in my ears, it was off to Australia for a gap year, and the first and only season of my life without mounted hunting.

CHAPTER 4

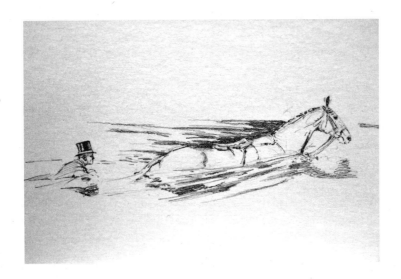

Australia, Cirencester and beyond

I was not overly concerned about friends, family or home when packed off to Australia to become a jackaroo, for the biggest wrench was to miss an entire season's hunting and winter forays after all kinds of game with Boozer. Thankfully I arrived in Sydney with Ian Burr's contact details tucked into my pocket, which had been provided by the Newcastle and District beagles' huntsman, Peter Howe. Ian worked as the dog catcher in the Sydney suburb of Blacktown and also maintained a bobbery pack of hounds that he hunted on foot in the Blue Mountains at every opportunity. A couple of months after my arrival I caught the night train down from Armidale to Sydney and joined him for a weekend that began with several friends loosing off their mixed pack of harriers, foxhounds and beagles at sunset.

Gathered around a blazing camp fire with the rugged mountains as a backdrop and a crate of Tooheys to hand, we swapped hunting stories all night long to the background music of hounds running in full cry through the scrubby foothills. They were still going strong at first light the following morning, which was our cue to grab a shotgun and head off into the bush to try and ambush a hare, fox, wallaby or larger wallaroo. After two consecutive days and nights, hounds returned to the campsite for a good feed before the journey home, during which Ian revealed that any unclaimed stray dog remotely resembling a hound would always be given the chance to join his unique working pack.

I enjoyed several more outings with Ian Burr and, being quite unaware that organised hunting flourished in Victoria, often thought how well a pack of foxhounds would fit in to the high New England grasslands surrounding Armidale where I was working on a merino sheep station. A move north to Queensland presented the opportunity to hunt wild pigs with strong bull-terrier crossbreds that hung on fiercely to their quarry's ears, and some exciting rough shooting where the bag was as varied as it was large. On one such outing I slayed a magnificent dog fox, and despite being thousands of miles from the nearest hunt, felt such remorse and guilt that I have never lifted a gun to one since, wherever in the world I might be. I arrived back in England in time to join the Goathland Hunt on a spring foot day from Egton Bridge and the news that my father was taking over as master on 1 May following Jamie Cameron's resignation.

Later that year I joined the fresh intake of students at the Royal Agricultural College, which seemed to be the best option of further education for a young man with aspirations to hunt a pack of foxhounds, for, like Stowe, the RAC also maintained a pack of beagles for the benefit of its students. I was at once invited to whip in to Simon Richardson, along with my new contemporary, Simon Hart, who had hunted the beagles at Radley. With his father, the MFHA secretary Anthony Hart, living nearby, this was very much Hart territory, and there was an inevitability to Simon's subsequent appointment as master, a role that he discharged with dedication and enthusiasm. We remained firm friends, even sharing a house one year that was provided by my godfather at Barnsley Park, but after a season in green I was ready to move on from beagling at Cirencester. The RAC beagles were racy and ruthless hare catchers, but a twenty-minute burst could never match the classic ninety-minute runs we so frequently enjoyed at Stowe. I saw Simon again in South Pembrokeshire in the winter of 2016, where we were guests on a rough and ready woodcock shoot, and was heartened to discover that the MP and former Chief Executive of the Countryside Alliance has lost none of his enthusiasm for the chase. We spent the day peeling off the main drives to hunt out thick double banks with our gundogs, and at lunchtime Simon showed me images of huge wild trout he had landed the previous summer.

That I was able to move seamlessly from whipping in to the beagles to hunting several days a week was thanks in no small part to the kindness of the late Gilly Scott, who owned a tough and reliable cob named Scally. Gilly's husband, Martin, was sharing hunting the VWH hounds with my childhood hero, Sidney Bailey, and I was offered Scally to hunt in exchange for some mucking out and exercise. Both huntsmen were kind enough to send me off on point all day long, and I soon came to appreciate the varied delights of the VWH's expansive four days a week country. The longest hunts were often achieved across the huge arable enclosures and light Cotswold brash soil of the Saturday country, but the best fun was to be had on Wednesdays and Thursdays around Oaksey, Highworth and Purton Stoke where rough pastures and thick vale hedges provided foxes and excitement in equal measure. The VWH is particularly fortunate to include the glorious Cirencester Park in their Monday country, where extensive mixed woodlands and wonderfully supportive owners combine to make this landscape a true test of the foxhound and a delight for all lovers of venery.

I also had a memorable season with the Beaufort, where Captain Ian Farquhar had recently arrived from the Bicester and Warden Hill to hunt hounds and where Major Ronnie Dallas was still the hunt secretary. The Beaufort charge subscribers by the horse, but Ronnie allowed me and Roddy Ando, to whom I had whipped in at the Stowe beagles a few years earlier, to share one horse on a generous student subscription. Guinness was stabled with Sue Godwin at Wick Farm near Didmarton; Sue now runs a busy livery yard that probably has a very long waiting list, but in 1985 Roddy's Irish hunter was the sole paying guest at her parents' grass farm. Ian Farquhar still talks fondly of the day when Guinness swam the River Avon from Dauntsey with me hanging on to his tail, and how attempting to follow us was what he jokingly refers to as one of his biggest mistakes in hunting. 'I was riding a good mare called Winslow Girl that came from David Barker', he reminded me only last season at the end of a wet Beaufortshire Monday. 'She couldn't get out of the river, and for the rest of her life would never go near water again. What made it even worse was that there was a bridge less than five hundred yards away.'

I soon had the chance to hunt many more horses, including a chestnut pointer belonging to great train robber turned car dealer, Eric Cordery, who offered the ride having sold me a car from his yard just outside Cirencester. I also hunted horses belonging to Monday farmers Betty and John Crewe, Mary Wilson and Annie Backhouse, who had been a European champion showjumper and farmed with her husband at South Farm, home to the lovely Saturday covert of Snowstorm Gorse. By the time Marcus Armytage and I had moved into Chris and Alex Mason's stone cottage in Ablington, I was also riding out two or three lots of racehorses every morning for my new landlords and Michael Henriques at nearby

Winson. The permit holder's small but quality yard sent out many NH winners under the direction of head girl Nancy Clarke, whose parents loved hunting and were farming tenants of the Co-op nearby. Marcus went on to win the Grand National on Mr Frisk in 1990 and made many of us proud to call him our friend that day; he loved his hunting too and was a frequent visitor to the Sinnington before becoming a joint master of the Old Berks in 2000.

When Martin Scott retired, Captain Fred Barker took on the mastership with Sidney remaining as sole huntsman. Known from his days as the Quorn Monday MFH as something of a martinet, Captain Fred invested time and money into his new challenge, and was a fearless field master across a country that was often much hairier than high Leicestershire. I found myself on the wrong side of Fred during the last vale day of the 1986 season when hounds met at Minety and the large field included several visitors from Leicestershire with high expectations of a good day. As hounds left the meet to draw Fishponds, I went on point as usual with Joe Collingborn, and the pack was soon streaming away across rough pastures and unkempt hedges. I was riding a hitherto unremarkable pointer belonging to Christine Mason called Bruce, who when confronted by a huge black hedge, set his jaw, raced at the enormous obstacle and soared over in quite the most spectacular leap of his life. I have jumped a few decent hedges since, nearly all of them forgotten by the next fence, but that mammoth obstacle remains the largest place I have ever got across intact. With so much excitement it was not until the hunt petered out at Red Lodge that Sidney, Joe or myself realised we had been without the field for the entire forty-minute run.

We were soon reminded of this unpalatable fact by gleeful foot followers lining the roads on the way back to where the second horses were waiting – Fred had introduced the Leicestershire habit of changing at a pre-determined location – who were quick to point out that the master's famously short fuse had comprehensively blown. Not just his, as it transpired, for the entire field looked furious as we rode up on weary, mud-splattered horses in marked contrast to the ranks of spotless, gleaming hunters that were waiting champing at the bit. Christine Mason, uncharacteristically for the Yorkshire-bred horsewoman I thought, also failed to see the sporting side of our adventure and told Diana Trotter to jump on my second horse whilst I took Bruce home. As is so often the case with those who have a quick temper, all was quickly forgiven and I later returned to hunt as Fred's guest on a particularly fine chestnut of his called Hector.

Towards the end of my time at Cirencester, Roddy Ando resurfaced in Somerset, where he was living with a lady called Claudia and subscribing to the Blackmore and Sparkford Vale. An invitation to join them for a weekend led to friendship with Rob Cursham, a brave horseman who hunted those hounds with quiet determination. I enjoyed several good days riding his daughter's small, grey mare called Souvenir, who made light of enormous black hedges jumped from hock-deep mud. This was a classic vale country where the thick hedges were small coverts in their own right and the hunting was fast, furious but often short-lived. I decided it was an easy country in which to thrill the subscribers but a hard one in which to catch a beaten fox, or achieve the long hunts that are the holy grail of foxhunting.

Failing my law exam at Cirencester extended this carefree existence by another whole year, although I spent a season working for NH trainer, Jimmy Fitzgerald, in Malton where Forgive 'N Forget was being prepared to win the 1985 Cheltenham Gold Cup. Most of the lads addressed the trainer as 'Guv' to his face and 'Fitzy' behind his back, but what I remember best from my time at Norton Grange was being told by the highly successful trainer that he would rather win a Waterloo Cup than a Grand National. Jimmy Fitzgerald did not win the world's greatest steeplechase or the blue riband of the leash, but amongst other prestigious races he did train Androma to win the Scottish Grand National twice; he was fond of reminding us that he also led up the winner of the same race as a young Irish stable lad before riding Brasher to victory in 1965. Afternoons were devoted to hunting rabbits with my fellow stable lads and the Norton Grange bobbery pack that consisted of terriers, lurchers and whippets. Summers were spent working at the Fasig Tipton, Keeneland and Saratoga thoroughbred yearling sales in the USA, although I was always back in time for the start of autumn hunting. After a September morning with the Beaufort from Chavenage, Ian Farquhar invited me to his home at Happylands for breakfast; over bacon and eggs he told me that it was now high time I took on a pack of hounds myself – and as it happened he knew just the place.

CHAPTER 5

First season on Dartmoor

Ten days later I found myself riding behind the Spooners and West Dartmoor from Mary Tavy as they drew up a steep gorse-strewn valley that was full of foxes. The day ended at Tavy Cleave, a plunging ravine scattered with granite boulders the size of cars, which must surely qualify as the roughest country hunted from the back of a horse anywhere in Britain. The followers were friendly, the hounds accurate and the country wilder and more beautiful than anywhere I had ever hunted before. Shortly after my visit a letter arrived from the secretary of the Spooners Hunt informing me that I had been appointed to join Tim Millar in the mastership from 1 May 1987, with full responsibility for hounds and kennels. I would never have felt confident enough to look after a pack of hounds – in fact two packs, for my charges that first season included the Devon & Cornwall mink hounds – single-handedly had it not been for Nat Thornton at Stowe; under his tutelage I had learnt how to manage hounds on and off the hunting field and skin a sheep or calf in two minutes flat.

Shortly before my arrival on Dartmoor the late Frank Toye, a huge, kind man who worked for Devon County Council, kept racing pigeons and loved following hounds by car, had a bit of an altercation with a past master in the lavatory after a particularly heated committee meeting. The press were quick to add lustre to the story by describing the Spooners as one of Prince Charles's favourite hunts; this was hardly accurate reporting, however, HRH's Duchy of Cornwall was our biggest landowner by some way and, I was soon to discover, also the supplier of the kennel's water. This cost the hunt a shilling a year in rent and was taken from a moorland leat via an inch-wide hole bored centuries earlier through solid granite. The sparkling trickle of life-giving water sustained hounds, horses and myself for three years without ever once freezing over, although the tiny and distant hole became so frequently clogged with bracken during dry, windy days of high summer that I eventually purchased a trials bike for the daily unblock.

My new home sat with its back to the very edge of Dartmoor, but faced inland across a patchwork of small, green fields divided by ragged Devon banks and wooded hollows of beech, holly, oak and thorn. I discovered a jackdaw's nest in the kitchen range on my first evening, and piles of pornographic magazines left behind by the previous occupant, who was clearly not thrilled to be leaving paradise. Their place was taken by a red coat the former Meynell master and close family friend, Dermot Kelly, had given me on learning of my new appointment. The coat fitted me like a glove and lasted for many long seasons. When I opened the door of the kennel's cold store the following morning, I was confronted by a grey wall of rotting bibles stacked fifteen deep from floor to ceiling. Otherwise known as rumens, bibles are the first component of a cattle's stomach, capable of holding up to 50 gallons of partially digested feed amongst so many folds of membrane that they are compared to pages of a Bible.

One of my tasks was to visit the abattoir in Tavistock several days a week and collect as many bibles as I could heave into the back of the hunt's battered old Land Rover with a pitchfork. I quickly learnt not to feed the green balls of slime on concrete yards, but to spread them about the small grass paddock for hounds to break up after exercise. Bibles put a sheen on hound's coats, and fed this way ensured that the grass was waist-high by the end of April. But bibles alone were not sufficient to sustain a pack of foxhounds. Raw flesh was needed for that, and there was no shortage in a land devoted almost entirely to livestock. The old adage, where there is livestock you will have deadstock, was repeated to me so many times that first summer that it became a mantra to be regurgitated for the benefit of anyone who asked how I was getting on in my new role as an MFH.

Walking hounds out that first morning down a quiet, high-banked, grassy lane was the most sublime of experiences; Tim Millar, Mike Doidge and I stood beneath the ancient church at Sampford Spiney where the four granite pinnacles have been dappled grey-green by centuries of creeping lichen, and watched hounds feathering about the close-cropped green. I marvelled then, as I still do, how quickly and comprehensively a pack of hounds places their trust and obedience with a new master in a manner that is humbling and gratifying in equal measure. Those who have never worked with hounds often find it astonishing that their keepers are able to distinguish one from another, although I have always been able to remember hounds and dogs much better than people. Recognising hounds is not just a matter of colour and conformation; it is also to do with the mannerisms, gait and demeanour that combine to make up an individual hound.

As I cast my eye over my new pack I could pick out the handsome quartet of Hampshire, Hazard, Hector and Herdsman '86, quality tan-and-blue mottle dogs that could have won a two-couple prize in the show ring; Major '83 with his dark, flecked neck, coy Dormouse '85, Crafty '83 dark as night and the lemon-and-white sisters, Gingham, Gorgeous and Gracious '84. Siblings Demon and Darling '83 were there too; Berkeley-bred, they were two of the finest hounds it has ever been my privilege to hunt. Darling was pure white save for a lemon patch over her right ear, whilst her striking tricolour brother commanded attention, even when just walking out. Demon went off his feet on the way back from autumn hunting one morning and, fearing the worst, we fastened him up in a farmer's stable for collection later. When I got back to the kennels, Demon was waiting there, having torn down the door and beaten us home across the moor. Equally prominent was Carpenter '82, an enormous lemon-and-white dog severely over at the knee, but possessed of such a fine nose that he could own the line of a fox for hours after it had gone. Many a fine hunt was to get under way with Carpenter's deep booming voice ringing out across the moor as he single-handedly unravelled an overnight drag.

The pack included an attractive blue mottle bitch from the Duke of Beaufort's called Radiant '85 that Ian Farquhar had given me, along with the unentered Crowner and Croaky. It is sometimes said amongst huntsmen that no one ever gives a good hound away, but Ian's gift of Radiant was typically generous. Not only was she a looker – her litter sister had won the brood bitch class at Peterborough – she was also a sound and reliable hunter that I came to trust implicitly. Radiant distinguished herself within weeks of starting hunting by slamming into a big dog fox at Radge Quarry after an evening foot meet in September. Crowner and Croaky went on to become fine hounds too, but Martin Scott's gift of the unentered Galaxy went horribly wrong when the tan bitch with smouldering, amber eyes went missing after a morning's cubhunting at Mary Tavy and was never seen again.

The area is littered with mine shafts and there is little doubt as to what became of the lovely young bitch. The thought of her grisly fate haunts me to this day.

Despite having realised the ambition of my dreams, I still drove back to Gloucestershire on 2 May to ride Singing the Blues and Hung Dial in the Berkeley Hunt point-to-point at Stone. The latter horse ran a good race to be third in division two of the maiden, beaten by Julian Smyth-Osborne and Alan Hill. Driving back past Sourton Tors with the western fringe of the moor glowing in evening light felt like coming home, and I could hardly wait to see the hounds and check that they had been well looked after in my absence. They were fine, of course, but I realised as I looked into the crowd of waving sterns and deep, trusting eyes that disappearing off to ride in point-to-point races was not really something of which they approved. So I stopped, and never rode in a race again.

Non-hunting days on Dartmoor were spent gathering deadstock from farms scattered about the Spooners' country, which extended as far west as the Okehampton road, north to the remote and inaccessible heart of the moor, east to the Princetown road and south to Plymouth. There were no mobile telephones in 1987, which meant that messages were relayed via a dirty white answerphone that frequently became too full to accept any more. Deciphering rich Devonian accents was somewhat challenging to begin with, and on more than one occasion I had to prevail on Mike Doidge to come and interpret for me. Mike farmed a few fields away from the kennels at Wilsetton, whipped in wearing a red coat and provided invaluable help whenever it was needed. His saintly wife, Wendy, took care of my washing for the full three years of my time on Dartmoor.

The flesh round was conducted in the old hunt Land Rover and wooden trailer fitted with a hand winch capable of hauling on board a ton or more of dead cow. During lambing and calving times in spring, this daily task sometimes lasted until dark, and that was just the picking up. Every animal had to be skinned, gutted and butchered for the hounds, although the skinny moor jocks with pallid flesh the texture of firm jelly invariably found their way straight into the bins, which were emptied, no questions asked, on a weekly basis. In those days the skin of every farm animal had a price, and it was a matter of both honour and financial necessity that no carcase was ever disposed of without first removing its skin. These were stacked and salted down one on top of another according to species, the different piles weeping silently on the flesh house floor as they awaited collection by the hide merchant from Cornwall.

The service offered to farmers included euthanasia of sick or injured animals, meaning that I was required to take possession of the hunt's .32 humane killer and apply for a firearms certificate to accompany it. A slight hiccup involving pheasants, my late friend Mike St Aubyn and an air rifle at Cirencester meant that I was temporarily prohibited from possessing a firearm, although I had since become friendly with the magistrate responsible for this unhappy state of affairs. I am forever grateful to Lord Oaksey for writing to the Devon and Cornwall constabulary on *Daily Telegraph* headed paper and explaining that he had not really meant to fine us at all, and that possessing a firearm was crucial to my new and important position. My certificate arrived just in time, and his Lordship duly came down to Dartmoor and spoke of his racing and hunting exploits at our Opening Meet dinner a few months later.

Running a flesh round presented the perfect opportunity to get to know the farmers whose land we hunted across, for heaving rotten sheep into the trailer wearing leggings and wellie boots went down well with men who eked a hard living from an unforgiving landscape. Within a few days of my arrival I was asked by Mary Ann and John Furze to collect a bullock from their small farm on the banks of the Tamar. The beast had expired at the foot of a steep cliff, and Mary Ann had already carved the carcase into several rough pieces by the time I arrived; each lump was then fastened to a rope, which was in turn tied to a harness fitted on to a tough, dun cob named Orbit and slowly dragged up on to the field above. This was my first introduction to a wonderfully resourceful, kind and mustard-keen hunting family that typified the Spooners Hunt. The following spring I sent Gingham over to their farm to whelp, but she unfortunately aborted the entire litter. When I called to collect her I was surprised to find Mary Ann cooking up the still-born puppies on the kitchen Aga. 'Couldn't let so much protein go to waste,' was all she said, although I understood the meat was destined for her sheepdogs and not her husband.

When not attending to the flesh round, skinning or exercising hounds, I spent as much time as possible exploring my new hunting country on horseback, accompanied by young moorland farmers such as Peter Heard, Jed Watson or Will Hutchins. In their company I rode high into the quivering, boggy depths of the moor, and learnt how to reach the faraway summit of Fur Tor by riding up the stony bed of moorland streams, following sheep trods through the mires or creeping along Phillpotts Pass, an 8ft-deep sunken trench with a floor firm enough to carry the sturdiest hunter. I still have the much-thumbed and grimy Ordnance Survey map on which I meticulously recorded the way in and out of every bog, valley, marsh and swamp in the Spooners country with a combination of lines, dots and crosses. This knowledge was to stand me in good stead during winter, for there are few worse sensations than being on board a horse as it starts to sink slowly into the mire. Several times I saw horses wallowing helplessly up to their withers in slime, and a whip laid hard over the hindquarters to galvanise the monumental effort needed to stagger free from a fate worse than death.

A paradise that is the Walkham Valley lies less than five hundred yards from the kennels: an extraordinary broken and beautiful wilderness littered with giant rocks, ancient trees draped in beards of green lichen, and in summer, great rafts of bracken to smother a multitude of glades and clearings a verdant green. Before the bracken takes proper hold, hillsides glow with the azure tinge of a million bluebells, and the churning white Walkham rushes dramatically downstream in a series of foaming rapids, plunging waterfalls and clear, quieter pools where the salmon and sea trout congregate. Charlie and Carrie Lawson came to live amongst these Tolkienesque surroundings at Heckwood, a granite-built house of great antiquity where a cavernous fireplace stretched the full width of their living room. The Lawsons became great friends; Carrie was unfailingly game on every kind of horse, and with a black patch over his right eye, Charlie made for a distinguished and generous host. He used to say that he always knew when I had called in for a coffee by the all-pervading smell of flesh that lingered for hours after my departure.

The smell was thoroughly scrubbed off in July when James Daly invited me to judge his Ledbury puppy show with Captain Simon Clarke, where the kennel huntsman, Andrew Elliot, moved hounds about the ring with consummate ease. James had provided me with my first point-to-point winner three years earlier, but sent me back to Dartmoor with something even more special than Bright Beacon's win at Maismore: a small, tricolour bitch called Celebrate '84, who sat on the back seat of my car all the way home and turned out to be another draft hound to confound the sceptics. On New Year's Day my final season, we had a remarkable two-and-a-quarter-hour hunt all about the Walkham Valley that was saved when Celebrate carried the line joyously, confidently and alone for several hundred yards along the disused railway track below Swell Tor. No other hound was able to join in until the fox headed out across open moorland, after which he was caught at Rundlestone, close to Princetown prison.

Mounted hound exercise was in full swing by the start of July and with help of local plasterer, Graham Goddard, Mike Doidge and his daughter, Tracy, I was able to take hounds amongst sheep morning after morning after morning, until I felt confident enough to slip into Merrivale Newtake soon after daybreak and encourage hounds to draw where I knew they would find a fox. They caught one too; a cloud of steam rose from the rocks where Farmer '84 had nailed his quarry after rattling around the grey slopes of Great Mis Tor for twenty heavenly minutes. I had to dig out the next fox myself after hounds had run it to ground in a small hole at the edge of Eggworthy Wood at the end of our first official morning's hunting. I waited whilst Mike rode half an hour home for my black and tan terrier, Spooner, spade and gun, then left me happy as a sandboy to complete my task surrounded by green bracken, clear blue skies and a pack of hounds eager for their reward.

The Opening Meet is a significant event for every hunt, a time of anticipation, excitement and a sense of achievement in having reached an important milestone of the hunting year. No huntsman will ever forget his first. I remember a busy morning all about Pork Hill in warm October sunshine, and much later a fox from Langstone Bog heading out across the open moor. Hounds were still running him ninety minutes later, although I had by then traded my weary second horse for Sue Sprott's rangy thoroughbred, Just a Kinsman. Our fox turned back from the Princetown road in the cool of late afternoon with the pack flying so fast in his wake that I had to get after Sue's valiant blood horse to stay in touch. When hounds run like that across clean ground on a burning scent it is inevitable that the youngest will pull to the front, and as I rounded the shoulder of Staple Tor I could see the pack well strung out with three or four first-season hounds clear of the rest and travelling like racing greyhounds over the rocky sward. Bumbling along in front of them was a bunch of scraggy moorland sheep going as fast as their spindly black legs could carry them.

Six months earlier I had opened a letter of welcome from Captain Mike Howard MC, who had enjoyed a long and successful mastership of the Spooners. He offered help where it was needed and warned me to be wary of sheep. 'Your critics – and all Masters have them', he wrote, 'will be looking for you to chase the local scotch sheep, and they can be buggers'. His words were ringing in my ears as, powerless to intervene, I watched the young hounds draw rapidly closer to the fleeing sheep, which at the very last moment peeled off down the hill to reveal the beaten fox that had been running amongst them. Minutes later I was picking my way off Staple Tor surrounded by happy hounds with his mask swinging from my saddle. I can only imagine what the foot followers watching from Merrivale quarry far below must have been thinking as the drama unfolded, but my appearance amongst them was greeted only by broad smiles and a whisky bottle proffered in the gloaming.

It felt as though all my Christmases had come at once that year, for the season was open, foxes came readily to hand – including a memorable two brace caught above ground from Postbridge – and the dreaded fog had been largely forgiving. My first glance on a hunting morning was always towards the high ground of Pew Tor, for I knew that it could spell disaster if its rocky summit was shrouded in mist. Occasionally the fog came down so suddenly out hunting that there was nothing for it but to pack up and go home, with or without hounds, which unfailingly made their way back to the kennels. Every time I went up to the yard I would find a few more hounds curled up asleep in the hay barn; they were nearly always all back by 10 p.m., and no hound ever came to mishap in this way. Whenever possible, we stayed out until the onset of dusk, at which point Charles Doughty, who worked as a divorce lawyer in London but maintained a lovely Devonian base at Denham Bridge, would invite any survivors to dine with him at the sumptuous Horn of Plenty in a few hours' time. This kind man offered an elegant chest of drawers when I first moved into the unfurnished kennels house, and presented me that first Christmas with a generous voucher to be spent at Creebers, which was, and still is, Tavistock's answer to Fortnum and Mason. I have never appreciated a Christmas present more.

CHAPTER 6

More tales from the Spooners

Our season finished with a lambing call at the end of April, a tally of 34½ brace and the same two horses that had started hound exercise ten long months earlier. This was a credit to the Chairman's wife, Jan Ross, who kept them at livery once the first early mornings were out of the way. Jan was naturally protective of her charges, and we crossed swords on more than one occasion as a result, most fiercely during a day when George Turner had agreed to mount me so the two hunt horses could be given a well-deserved rest. George is a rough, tough and fearless horseman with a bent back, grey hair and a face like a Brillo pad, who was still race riding as a comprehensively battered sixty-year-old. His speciality was winning races with horses bought out of Ascot sales for peanuts. The idea was that every horse I rode would need one fewer day to qualify as a fairly hunted pointer, but I had not fully grasped the extent of George's cunning plan that day.

The first horse was a magnificent-looking bay gelding called Swillbrook Lad that George had bought for a song at Ascot sales the previous week; magnificent-looking but so unfit that his replacement was being lined up before we had even found a fox amongst the bracken and in-bye country surrounding Pound Down. By 1 p.m. I was hunting hounds from George's third string, which unlike Swillbrook Lad was not produced in a hunting saddle and preferred to go backwards rather than forwards, although Bishopric was destined to go on and become a successful point-to-pointer. As I jumped into the flimsy racing plate I overheard Jan say in a very loud and, it has to be said, very horsey voice, 'Oh look, he's knackered that one already'. She really should have ignored my bark to go home, but off she went and was not seen again that week.

The day was not done yet for Jo Miall rode up around 3 p.m. and asked if I would like to ride Waggie as she was languishing in a nearby field. I already knew all about Waggie. The 15.3 bay mare with an unusually high action used to win midnight steeplechases for fun, and on more than one occasion had hurtled past me out hunting with Jo – who was a leading point-to-point jockey – quite unable to stop. I accepted without hesitation, and when Jo appeared leading a very muddy and shaggy Waggie, I handed the last budding racehorse back to a bemused George Turner. I settled into her saddle like the proverbial seagull on the sand, trotted off to draw a field of kale, found a fox and ran hard for half an hour or more over a succession of five-bar gates. Seldom have I enjoyed a hunt more than that quick evening thing from Crapstone. I took Waggie back to the kennels in the dark and there she stayed, for when Jo and her boyfriend came to collect her much later that evening I offered them the brown envelope left under the salt tub by the hide man from Liskeard. Jo took the flesh money without counting the contents, but I think we both got a good deal.

The hunt provided me with two stalwart horses in Justin and Floyd, the first a clever chestnut that made light of the tallest Devon banks, the second a tough and gutsy liver chestnut that consistently gave of his all. I also acquired a handy black gelding named Sultan after his owner sent him to the kennels to be shot. I could never fathom out why, for he turned out to be a steady and reliable spare horse. Other horses that passed though the stables at Sampford Spiney included a magnificent Irish hunter with the onset of pedalostitis that had originally come from Dr Tom Connors' famous yard at Muxloe Hill in Leicestershire. Dartmoor was hardly the country for a horse of Galaxy's calibre but the ubiquitous soft going extended his life by a season or two. I bought General Lee for a pittance at Ascot sales and sent him down to Heckwood to be educated by Carrie Lawson – I am not sure he ever came back – and recall a rangy, grey horse named Conjob that lived up to his name.

Towards the very end of my first season a scruffy young man appeared at the kennels having walked a mile up the road from his council house home at Brook. Alan Hughes had a natural affinity with hounds and before long was helping out at the kennels, but the real challenge was to teach him how to skin. I left him with half a dozen sheep to deal with whilst I took hounds over to Postbridge for the closing meet in mid April, but when I returned there were still four to go. He gradually became more proficient, and a real help during busy times of year, although he possessed a mind-boggling talent for the telling of tall stories. He was very rarely late for work, but the excuse that he had been swept down to the Tamar estuary having fallen in whilst poaching salmon many miles upstream did not really wash.

Alan was the only person ever paid to help out, but many others gave their time freely and generously to support the hunt. Kevin Ellicott was broad-shouldered with wavy, silver hair and a weather beaten face that bore testament to countless hours spent up on the high moor, where he put out red warning flags whenever the military were training. He kept a pony for this purpose, which was exchanged for a Land Rover on hunting days when Kevin and his friend, Ron McCoy, did the terrier work. Kevin knew the moor backwards, and was able to tell me the whereabouts of many litters born up on the ranges, including one breed that shifted a dead pony more than five hundred yards closer to their earth over a six-week period in May. It soon became obvious that even Kevin could not get to every mark quickly, especially if it was a long way from the nearest track. The solution was for Mary Ann to carry Spooner in a bag slung around her shoulder whilst riding Orbit, and in this way our hunting improved beyond measure. Roughly half the foxes we ever found on the high moor were laid to ground amongst the jumbles of rocks that litter the slopes of every tor on Dartmoor, but they were seldom very far in, and usually left at speed when faced by a terrier.

Spooner and Mary Ann became a much valued team who between them were responsible for countless good hunts that we would otherwise have missed. Spooner became so adept at his job that having bolted a fox he would select a suitably high rock from which to jump back on to the pommel of Orbit's saddle. Occasionally things did not go to plan, as on the December afternoon when I rode off the moor in shirtsleeves having left my red coat folded up amongst the rocks at Sharp Tor. The place was too remote to return to that evening, but I was there at first light, tramping uphill beneath a blueing sky and remembering Glaisdale Head more than a decade earlier. Spooner was shivering in his sleep on top of my stiff red coat, but none the worse for his lonely night on the moor.

Fur Tor – said to be a corruption of Far Tor – is the most remote and least accessible place on Dartmoor, but in those days there was still plenty of stock on the high moor, and foxes to feed off any that did not survive. Mike Howard used to meet there on 1 May each year, often catching a fox or two on the way, and although I never emulated that feat, the policy of drawing towards Fur Tor from every moorland meet was a recipe for exciting hunting. Hounds marked in a peat hag up there late one afternoon when Frank Houghton-Brown was deputising for Mary Ann on Orbit. I was not convinced that allowing my terrier into an unknown earth in the most remote point of southern England with nightfall just around the corner was particularly sensible, but Frank was of the opposite persuasion. Spooner went in, out came the fox and away went the hounds in full cry, all except for South and West Wilts Vision '85, which Simon Clarke had given me after she became too sharp for a vale country and started ambushing foxes like a lurcher. He believed she would find this trick difficult on open moorland, and so it had proved up until now. As the rest of the pack chimed away after their quarry, the broken-coated Vision stood and waited a few long seconds to appraise the situation before racing off at right angles and intercepting the fox with lethal accuracy as he picked his way back uphill through the boulders.

Dartmoor had its problems, of course, in common with every other hunting country in Britain, but with virtually no shooting to contend with, a plentiful supply of foxes and hardly a farm in the country that hounds were not welcome across, there were few distractions to prey on a huntsman's mind. John Cole from Chaddlehanger once gunned down a fox in front of hounds, but the deed was motivated by the stockman's hatred of a predator and not by any grievance against the hunt. Even though the fox was shot on his own land, the farmer was anxious to depart the scene as quickly as possible, and were it not for the loud retort, gunsmoke hanging in the air, and his broad back disappearing into a thick hedge, may well have accomplished his task undetected. His intervention made no difference to the hounds, which broke the fox up as if they had caught it themselves. I have seen him many times since, but neither one of us has ever mentioned the incident. Another hill farmer used to snare and shoot foxes on sight, remove their valuable pelts and then drop the skinned carcases at the kennels to be disposed of. As he saw no irony attached to this procedure, it rattled me far less than when in later life I came across foxes that had been slain and left out deliberately to goad and upset. Instead, I merely marvelled at how tiny a fox looks with his thick red pelt removed.

By the end of three years I had made good friends on Dartmoor from all walks of life, amongst them the remarkable Anne and Art Cole, who lived in a cluster of caravans surrounded by the trappings of a small livestock farmer. Their thirteen children were all raised to ride, hunt and farm, although there was seldom enough cash for anything so fancy as a saddle. One of the youngest, Joanne, rode all day on the annual pony drift when just five years old, with nothing but a folded hessian sack to sit on. As a result each child grew up to be a consummate horseman or horsewoman with talents that could have been shaped into any equestrian discipline they chose, but instead they did as their parents had done before them, which was to marry locally and raise large families. Lambs, dogs and children often shared the same sleeping quarters, but the kids mucked in and helped as soon as they were old enough to walk. Such an environment seemed the perfect home for Carpenter to retire to after his honest brown eyes had sunk deep into their sockets and slime began to drip permanently from loose jowls. However, the sagacious old doghound had other ideas, and was back at the kennels within hours of being dropped off.

I sometimes ponder how life would have turned out had I stayed rooted to Dartmoor and set aside ambitions nurtured since childhood to hunt hounds in a glamorous jumping country. I knew I would never hunt a wilder landscape, but the ultimate call of the shires was impossible to resist, for ambition is the hallmark of youth, and at twenty-seven years old, to stay put on Dartmoor for the rest of my hunting career seemed too easy an option. During my third season at the Spooners, Colonel Nick Crossley – who had bred both Boozer and Spooner – was in touch to see if I would be interested in joining him in the Middleton mastership the following season. I thought back to Christmas Eve meets at Westow, and recalled a strange atmosphere that I could not quite place either then or now. I thanked the Colonel, declined his kind offer and suggested my friend Frank might be tempted. That union duly came to fruition and thus began a most successful era in the history of the Middleton Hunt. I felt differently about the neighbouring Sinnington when approached by them just a few weeks later. I had only fond memories of a hunt that has been described as one of the best two day a week countries in England, and quickly and happily agreed terms with their Chairman, James Holt, to take over the reins as sole master and huntsman from 1 May 1990.

Towards the end of my last season, it was the Spooners' turn to hunt at Two Bridges Hunt Club meet at the heart of Dartmoor. The club was formed in 1934 by hunting members of the Royal Navy at Dartmouth and is celebrated each year by a dinner followed by a hunt when the country of all four Dartmoor packs is traditionally made available for the day's sport. The dinner is attended by the great and good of the moor, wearing evening hunt dress, after which hand-painted menu cards depicting hunting scenes are auctioned off. I still treasure a small but charming watercolour as a memory of the evening, as well as a fine moorland run the following day out to Fernworthy Reservoir.

We had a bit of a do at the East Dart Hotel in Postbridge before I left, but I only remember Carrie Lawson having an altercation with the cattle grid as we staggered down the drive to Heckwood in the small hours. I began to dread the day when I would have to bid goodbye to hounds I had grown to love, for I was now on the ladder of progress, which for an amateur huntsman to the Sinnington meant employing someone else to look after the hounds. I knew then, with absolute certainty, that I would never be as close to a pack again; the guilt of their betrayal was overwhelming. The hounds had no such reservations, trotting along cheerfully with wise noses feeling the April breeze and sterns waving happily in the sunshine during my last precious hour with them alone. Back at the kennels the latch clicked shut, and I walked from those hounds with a heart of lead.

CHAPTER 7

A return to the North

The Sinnington is a near perfect hunting country with a wet, low-lying vale and a series of steep, wooded valleys running north to the moors neatly divided into two halves by a single main road. The wilder high side to the north of the A170 is hunted on a Saturday, whilst Wednesdays are devoted to the vale. The hill country's steep topography is ideal for showing high pheasants and is home to several large shooting estates, nearly all of which are helpful and accommodating to the hunt. The old-fashioned vale to the south is a land of many rivers, disparate farms, and quiet country lanes connecting small villages largely inhabited by people who were born and bred in Ryedale; but the jewels in the Sinnington's crown are the eleven thick thorn coverts strategically sited about the vale, which are owned and controlled by the hunt. Generations of Sinnington huntsmen have provided fast sport across the open, good scenting low country, and been able to retreat to the hills a few days later where foxes are harder to find, but hounds easier to settle in a terrain where the virtues of independence and persistence come to the fore.

I arrived in North Yorkshire on the last day of April to take up my appointment as sole master to the Sinnington Hunt accompanied by a distinctly run-up Waggie, a moor jock sheep, some terriers and a handful of hounds including my old friend Radiant and a young broken-coated bitch called Fairy '88, which I handed over to Albert Hickson at the kennels. Appointing the right kennel huntsman is one of the most important decisions an amateur will ever make, for the successful candidate must possess knowledge, skill, and an exceptionally high work ethic. He must also be able to cross country effectively on horseback, be good with people and, perhaps most crucial of all, he must be loyal to both the master and hunt that he serves. Albert had come to my attention via Charles Wheeler, who had by then replaced Brian Gupwell as Captain Farquhar's own kennel huntsman at Badminton. 'You must take Albert on', Charles had implored me. 'His wife is totally brilliant with horses.' Perhaps not the most important consideration when selecting your right-hand man, but Margaret was indeed a top-class stud groom – she now performs the same role at Badminton – and Albert was a popular and cheery soul who had to step down within two seasons to resolve an old knee injury.

That night I slept beyond earshot of hounds in my new cottage at Harome, which although only a tiny 'two up, two down' was to serve as a perfect base for the next eight seasons. Harome is a delightful village in the heart of the Sinnington vale, with broad twin verges of greenery separating stone built houses from the road, a discreet hotel and, in the Star Inn, a classic village pub with heavy, wooden beams, a coal fire in the grate and a cramped public bar. Pride of place was reserved for a very senior and long-retired shepherd, who drank from the same glass and sat on the same tall stool with his back to the wall each evening. When Andrew and Jacquie Pern transformed the pub by winning a Michelin star, wealthy foodies from West Yorkshire and beyond flocked to the tiny bar, but Ernest never once relinquished his seat, for he was as integral to the décor as the grimy fox and badger masks grinning down from the walls.

In November we met beneath a mighty oak tree opposite the pub, and in summer we bicycled with hounds up the quiet main street several mornings each week as the kennels were less than two miles distant. Pat Dodsworth, who came from a long line of farming and hunting stock, lay desperately ill one summer at Overdale Farm in the middle of the village, and we were able to walk hounds up to her bedroom window on the ground floor so that she could sit up in bed and enjoy the visit. There is a shallow pond at the far end of the village; hounds liked to plunge into its clear waters on warm summer mornings, often watched by guests breakfasting at the Pheasant Hotel. The village hall stood opposite my home at Primrose Cottage and was the domain of Tot Wardle, who organised weekly bingo sessions, including one every September for the benefit of the hunt. The fundraiser contributed little to the hunt coffers, but my greatest pleasure was the knowledge that my neighbours were so willing to support their local hunt. Tot was especially fond of walnuts and could be spotted collecting them in autumn from beneath farmer John Wilson's giant walnut tree in the next-door village of Nunnington. John sometimes followed the hunt in his Land Rover and still slept in the room that he was born in overlooking the yard at Jubilee Farm.

Unlike Dartmoor, North Yorkshire was a land of grand country estates and no shortage of equally grand personalities to occupy and enjoy them. Anne, Countess of Feversham, sat at the very top of the rural hierarchy and lived in isolated splendour at the remote but beautiful head of Bransdale in a magnificent Grade II listed house that, in common with nearly all the outlying farms, had once belonged to her late husband's family. The farms, Bransdale Lodge and some two thousand acres of land were gifted to the National Trust in lieu of death duties after the third Earl of Feversham died in 1963, but made available for his widow to live in for the latter part of her life. The Countess had been a master of the Sinnington for more than thirty years, during which time she rode side-saddle wearing a red coat, gained the adoration of numerous farmers and became the first lady to serve on the committee of the MFHA.

Anne very kindly and quickly took me under her wing; driving across wild moorland beneath spectacular sunsets on my way to dine at Bransdale Lodge became a frequent delight. I was thoroughly briefed over dinners served from a wheel-in trolley about all aspects of the Sinnington Hunt, and her sound advice that 25 per cent of the farmers were hugely supportive of hunting, a similar ratio difficult and the remainder ambivalent is probably as true today as it was nearly thirty years ago. During one such evening I noticed a silver hunting horn on the mantelpiece inscribed with the legend: 'This horn the property of the ruling master', and I drove back to Harome with it lying on the passenger seat beside me. I have little involvement with my old hunt nowadays beyond advising on hound breeding; however, I have made it my business to ensure that the silver horn from Bransdale Lodge is properly handed over at the end of each mastership. The Countess died during my fifth season with the Sinnington, and blowing her away following the funeral at Helmsley endures as one of my most poignant memories.

Major John Shaw was equally influential in the affairs of the hunt, and had for many seasons served alongside the Countess as a joint master, although by the time of my arrival he had not ridden for some years. His Welburn estate in the vale consisted of several well-sited and ideally sized coverts surrounded by a mix of arable and old pasture to complement the four becks that wend their way eastwards across the estate. There was a tiny connection in that the Major's mother had been my own mother's godmother, but I had never met the man who commanded a formidable reputation and who had not always seen eye to eye with my predecessor. Within a few weeks of my arrival in Yorkshire I received a handwritten note from the Major that began 'Dear Dangar', and went on to suggest a meeting soon after. During the subsequent summer afternoon we drove around the estate, which with burgeoning fields of ripening corn, gleaming green pastures, woodland in full leaf and fox cubs gambolling beside Bowforth covert, could not possibly have appeared more beguiling. We ended up sharing a bottle of chilled white wine at the Splash, a secret and spectacular water garden at the heart of the estate.

During that happy afternoon it was clear that access about the Welburn acres could be improved by the strategic siting of a few hunt jumps, but I never expected some twenty immaculate obstacles to have been built by the time hounds drew the estate just three months later, many of which are still standing to this day. That they appeared without fuss or further reference was typical of the Major's understated generosity, as was his invitation to roam anywhere I wished across Welburn with dog and gun, a gift that I made sure did not impact on his Christmas shoot, which was held the day after hounds had drawn the entire estate. We were invited to return to Welburn Manor for a lawn meet in December after a twelve-year absence, during which a lethal mix of cherry brandy and whisky, otherwise known as a Percy Special, was offered on a silver salver. I was not quite sure if I was seeing straight when Waggie popped over some rails into a newly planted covert behind Hall Farm soon afterwards and almost landed on top of a sleeping fox, which woke up quickly and just beat hounds into a land drain after a furious thirty minutes. Peter Easterby rode up at the end of the run and told me that me the new covert had been christened Coldwar, and that is the name it has gone by ever since. Two days later, eight of us shot a record bag of pheasants on the Welburn shoot.

Whenever I called in to visit John Shaw before a day's hunting I would be ushered into a quiet room off the kitchen where the Major liked to sit at his desk and read the *Daily Telegraph* with the aid of a long wooden stick to keep the pages in place. He would invariably lay the paper across his desk, cough like a starting tractor, light up a Players cigarette and, as the ash dribbled down the front of his bulging jersey, divulge some snippet of wisdom before we ever discussed the impending day's sport. The Major did not suffer fools gladly and there were some from within the hunt and his immediate circle that were immortalised by acid verse and caustic wit. 'Do you know what a thrush is?', he asked one morning, peering over his horn-rimmed glasses after we had discussed a tiresome lady in some detail. 'It's an irritating tw*t,', he explained, before I could suggest a lovely songbird and, from that day forward, the lady concerned went by no other name save 'The Thrush'.

Major Shaw's contempt for anyone he found pretentious, ignorant or stupid rarely extended to his neighbouring tenants and farmers, for like many others of similar station his distaste was reserved for the arriviste and anyone purporting to be something that they were not, perhaps best described as travelling under a false identity. The Brown family had been tenants at Welburn for generations, and were almost as involved in the Sinnington Hunt as their landlord had been in his capacity as master. Bill Brown served on the point-to-point committee for years and farmed to the north of Muscoates Whin, which was, and still is, the best hunt covert of them all. I was offered tea in a china cup and saucer whenever I visited, whilst the Browns' youngest son sat and glowered silently in the corner. Years later it was no surprise to learn that Andrew Brown's welcome to the hunt after his father died was at best lukewarm, although no one could ever understand why.

Bill's brother, Dick, farmed a pastoral paradise at West Ings in the low country from which base he bred, made and sold hunters all over England, most famously to Lord King from Leicestershire, whom I was destined to cross swords with many years hence. Dick and Bess invited friends and family to their cosy farmhouse after the annual Ryedale Show every July, where one of the glistening hams from the barn rafters would be cut into thick slabs of succulent perfection. Their grown-up sons, Michael and Richard, wolfed the meat down, ever mindful of their father's oft-imparted adage, 'slow at thou meat, slow at thou work'. Michael inherited his father's horsemanship but not his love of farming or livestock, so built a career around horses, hunting, point-to-pointing and shoeing.

Although never fat, Michael was a man of considerable substance, and beneath a stock of thick, black hair possessed the countryman's old-fashioned cunning that very rarely allowed either man or beast to get the better of him. He was also one of the finest heavyweight horsemen of his generation, guaranteed to be there at the end of the longest hunt, no matter how green or inexperienced his conveyance. Michael shod the hunt horses and freely imparted advice on all matters under the sun. When he thought that my friendship with a young lady was getting too serious I was cautioned: 'Before thou takes kitten, take a good look at t'owld cat'. I did just that, heeding his wise words.

Only a couple of miles stood between Michael's Wombleton home and Skiplam Grange in the high side, but the rambling stone farmhouse and surrounding land represented the different world of Nawton Tower estate, where the same families had farmed, walked hound puppies and been good friends to the hunt for generations. Bert Harper's flock of pedigree Suffolks at Skiplam Grange was his pride and joy; it was said that the old farmer kept the wealth they had reaped beneath the mattress of a rarely used bed. Bert once showed me his collection of cups, prizes and certificates won by his sheep at agricultural shows over fifty summers or more, proudly ushering me into a dim and crepuscular room crammed with faded trophies, cobwebs and dusty, grey furniture in a setting that evoked Miss Havisham's wedding feast. Bert lived in a downstairs room, slumbering throughout lambing time in a battered armchair beside rough-hewn logs smouldering on a foot of solid ash. Bonzo Skilbeck used to visit his friend on Sundays and roast a pheasant for lunch above the embers, although I don't think the fire was ever allowed to completely go out. After Bert's death his possessions – which included much fine, embroidered linen – and agricultural effects were auctioned off at a farm sale. Soon afterwards the builders moved in to transform the old farmhouse into a fine country residence that bears no resemblance to the dirty, humble dwelling I once knew.

Digby Fairbanks was also rumoured to keep a huge sack of money inside his house at Appleton-le-Street, which appeared derelict to motorists speeding past on the road between Hovingham and Malton. The sack was said to be so heavy that anyone capable of lifting it from the floor on would be allowed to keep the contents, but I cannot imagine Digby ever making such a rash offer. When the council asked the reclusive farmer to tidy up the exterior of the house, he responded by daubing shocking yellow paint all over the window frames, which made it look as though the house had been attacked by vandals. A neighbour from the village once sent his children round to Digby with mince pies for Christmas, and they returned with pockets bulging full of one-pound coins, which only served to fuel rumours of a huge sack of money within the house. A hippy lived in an old caravan hidden amongst thorns that had taken over Digby's neglected pastures to the north of the farmhouse, and shouted abuse at the hunt if we ever ventured too close for comfort.

Although I did not realise it at the time, Derek Jackson's warning a few weeks into my first season's cubhunting was one of the most astute pieces of advice I have ever been given on the hunting field. The silver-haired stockman waded up to my horse at Brawby through a sea of hounds, rested his gnarled hand on my breeched knee, and looked me clear in the eye. 'Just remember', he said, 'those that are your friends when you arrive will be your enemies when you leave'. I have still not worked out why that so often is the case, only that Derek's words will resonate with masters and huntsmen up and down the land. Less than a year earlier, his employer had stayed with me on Dartmoor, loved the wild hunting there and told me I was mad to be moving north. On arrival in Yorkshire I was urged by my former guest to buy and sell sheep at Malton market as a predecessor of mine had done; only I had no land on which to graze them, nor time to play at being a shepherd.

Within six months of my arrival in Yorkshire the same man started a petition amongst the Brawby farmers to protest against digging out foxes that had been run to ground, which like all petitions compiled under duress, was quickly forgotten – but not by me. Some seasons later, hounds enjoyed a fabulous morning amongst several foxes in the Brawby maize that ended with them marking in a tiny rabbit hole after two hours' continuous hunting. I wanted that fox, my hounds wanted that fox, but the landowner had forbidden me to dig. As it happens, he was standing less than a hundred yards from where hounds were eating soil in their determination to have their reward, surrounded by foot followers who I felt must surely be sympathetic to the pack's cause. 'You don't mind if we have this one, do you?', I asked. Ten minutes later the hounds went home happy.

Jeff Bean's farm stood beside the lonely, windswept lane that links the villages of Brawby, Salton and Great Edstone, where bold words beneath a Union Jack advised travellers that they had now left the EEC. 'Pints, gallons and acres only spoken here', the tall, black letters proclaimed. Although not a hunting man, the dairy farmer welcomed us across his land, like most of the Countess's ambivalent 50 per cent, because the hunt represented a rural way of life that he valued, liked and understood. Jeff's straw bales were a sure find in winter, but many years later the farmer inexplicably left and I have not seen him in the area since. The farm was sold and the small, brick house in which Mr Bean lived with apple orchard beside has been replaced by the grand façade of a country seat fashioned from gleaming Hovingham limestone that is much more compatible with the smart-sounding Salton Lodge address. Whenever I drive past I remember the scruffy farm as it once was, and Jeff Bean's comforting sign of defiance.

Salton Lodge takes its name from the sleepy backwater of Salton, a tiny village without shop or pub but home to a fine Norman church and half an acre of village green on which the Bentley family still host a popular meet. Wearing a black coat, Billy Bentley occasionally rode a home-bred hunter to hounds, but I saw more of the elegant farmer in early June, when huge trout stir from their lies in the Rivers Dove, Riccal and Rye that carve up the family farm to gulp down mayflies on balmy evenings that seem as if they will last forever. Billy sometimes appeared with his black-and-tan terrier at last light to admire my catch, and talk softly into the gloaming of the farm and land he loved so much. His brother, Robin, seldom felt the need to wander far from a place of such rare wildness and beauty, and shunned the company of all except those he knew well.

Despite this, there was a large turnout for his funeral in the old Norman church many years later, during which the vicar told us that Robin preferred livestock to machinery, enjoyed fishing and knew the run of local foxes better than any master of the hunt. His words took me back to a winter's day twenty years earlier when Robin had abandoned any discomfort he felt amongst strangers to confront me in a coat fastened at the waist with bailer twine, with orders to leave the fox that hounds had run to ground on his farm. After the service, earth pattered onto his wooden coffin like autumn rain, and I gave Robin's mother a photograph I had taken of her eldest son during mayfly time when he was still a young man. His face was smiling beneath a pork-pie hat that had a large grey mayfly perched on the side, the fair skin a little flushed with the heat of June. The backdrop in the photograph is a green sea speckled with grazing sheep, and later, at the pub where a huge spread was laid out for all comers, I saw Nancy showing the photograph to a huddle of curious well-wishers.

The desire amongst those who support the hunt to nurture and protect foxes is a dichotomy that outsiders often find hard to comprehend, however, feelings can run particularly high amongst men such as Robin Bentley, whose lives are rooted to the land. There are seldom any objections to a fox caught by hounds above ground, but amongst country folk there is sometimes real distaste for terrier work, which can be seen as unfair to a quarry that sustains a whole way of life in the countryside. When a fox was run to ground, huntsmen had to balance the needs of their hounds with the wishes of the relevant landowner and the wider fox population across the country they hunted. An effective and well-organised hunt had an important role to play in the management of foxes, and was the only method of control guaranteed to kill the sick and old ahead of the fit and healthy.

Many of the hunt coverts were looked after by men of Ryedale who would have sympathised with Robin's approach that day; these included the former terrierman, Keith Preston, who cared for Harome Whin as if it were his own wood, and who was left Father Walter Maxwell-Stuart's treasured 12-bore in the Ampleforth housemaster's will. A love of hunting runs deep in the Preston family, and Keith remembers to this day how his father and a fellow workman once downed tools as council roadmen to follow the Sinnington hounds during Penn Sherbrooke's mastership, and later helped to dig out the fox they had run to ground. Their reward from Mr Sherbrooke was a guinea apiece and a bottle of whisky to sup on the long walk home: remuneration that was equal to at least a fortnight's pay.

George Pilmoor Jackson, who had spent a lifetime working on the farming and sporting estate of Ness, once emptied half a can of diesel into an earth in Muscoates Whin rather than risk his beloved vixen being found below ground on a hunting day. George gave his middle name to a small covert that stands in front of the house I have called home for the last twenty years, although I had no idea that the young plantation would one day be mine when I drew it for the first time in September 1990. I remember Mrs Stamp dressed in a white smock driving her flock of geese to safety at our approach, and strong foxes that could not be contained. It is also a matter of record that the very last fox legally hunted in the Sinnington vale was found in Pilmoors covert in February 2005.

The owner of Ness, Hugh Murray Wells, had been responsible for planting and naming Pilmoors in the mid-1980s. Hugh was a true countryman, conservationist, lover of all field sports and, as I discovered much later, a poet of exceptional talent. Thanks to his generosity the hunt horses ate Ness-grown oats all winter, and enjoyed summer grazing in low-lying water meadows. When all around him were pocketing post-war grants to drain the low-lying vale for wheat production, the conservationist landowner put aside a long, narrow band of land between the tiny River Holbeck and the demming that mirrored its course and let nature do her work. The result was a diverse and habitat-rich wilderness known as Ness Grasses that was home to all kinds of fauna and wildlife and became one of the most reliable and remote coverts in the Sinnington vale. After his death the plough was called in to destroy in a few days much of what had taken a lifetime to establish; the sight of those beautiful grasses shorn short as common stubble troubles me still. Thankfully, much was spared, and to wander there in spring is still to hear the curlew's wild call, the whickering of fox cubs and the bark of a startled roe.

Just as John Shaw had shown me around Welburn, so Hugh gave me a tour of Ness that first summer, which is really a peninsular formed by the confluence of the Rivers Rye and Holbeck that could only be accessed by road from the west, although horses and humans on foot or cycle could reach Ness from the Bentleys' farm over a narrow gated iron bridge to the east, which Waggie and I once jumped on and off during a fast vale hunt. Hugh's home at Ness Hall included an extensive and beautiful garden and a number of ancient lime trees standing in parkland beyond, with their trunks circumnavigated by a mass of dense, green suckers a yard or more thick. Foxes liked to hide amongst the warm cover of two particular trees, although Hugh asked me that day only to try them following a lawn meet at his house. I learnt to scrutinise the base of these trees for tell-tale smudges of earth on the bark, which was a sure sign of regular vulpine use.

In Tange Pickard, the Sinnington Hunt claimed a foot follower who could climb trees as easily as any fox, for he had a favourite vantage point amongst the crown of a broad oak in Harome Whin from which to watch autumn hunting mornings unseen and undisturbed by any other follower. Tange's real name was Anthony, however, colleagues at the sawmill where he had worked in Helmsley used the diminutive of tangerine as reference to a mop of orange hair that had all but vanished by the time we first met. Skills acquired during a lifetime working with wood were put to good use in the creation of scores of skilfully crafted hunting gates that Tange generously donated to the hunt throughout my time as master, each one identifiable by his trademark T, fashioned from the metal of an empty baked-bean can. I seldom open a gate in the Sinnington Hunt country without inspecting the top beam for the Harome man's calling card, and smile in appreciation wherever it is found. Such was the land, and people I had come to live amongst.

CHAPTER 8

Hunting and shooting at the Sinnington

As well as meeting the Sinnington Hunt farmers and landowners, I made it my business to cultivate the friendship and support of the shooting community, especially those at the sharp end of a sport that was ousting hunting as the most popular rural pastime in Ryedale. Soon after my arrival in Yorkshire, Colonel Kit Egerton kindly paved the way by organising a convivial evening for gamekeepers and farmers to meet the new young master. There had been little organised shooting on Dartmoor, and foxes flourished accordingly, but it became apparent during an afternoon spent with the Duncombe Park head keeper, John Masterman, that I could not expect such bounties from the Sinnington high side. We travelled in his Land Rover to an expanse of wild forestry at the head of Beckdale known as Acre Grain, parked up and started to walk. Whenever we passed a puddle on the forestry track, John crouched low to inspect the soft peaty rim for the tell-tale sign of even a single fox print, and his eyes moved constantly about the verges, searching for the dry, white slugs of muck that every fox must leave behind. Later he examined a puff of brown feathers and identified the killer as a sparrow hawk, explaining that feathers from a fox kill are invariably glued together by saliva. I was thoroughly introduced to the powers of observation that summer afternoon and, in time, became as adept as any keeper in recognising foxy signs, however subtle they may be.

John proved to be a good friend to the hunt, and despite having day-to-day responsibility for one of the premier shoots in the country thought little of changing drives around in order to accommodate our interests. Although we sometimes ran on to his domain, he never expected hounds to be stopped and was always relaxed and understanding when contacted after the event. In turn, I made sure that we never drew a square yard of the Duncombe Park shoot without his say-so and, when running in, moved hounds on quickly once they checked, especially during the last hour of winter daylight when pheasants are contemplating their roosts for the night.

Duncombe Park's eastern boundary of Riccal Dale, a long, broad valley of ancient oaks, sunny glades and blocks of modern conifers, divided by the infant River Riccal, marched with the neighbouring Nawton Tower estate, which was owned by the Countess's daughter, Lady Clarissa Collin. Her land included the famous hunting valley of Skiplam, the largest and most spectacular of all the many dales that comprise the Sinnington high side, and a refuge for foxes that could be guaranteed no safe passage if they strayed north on to Bransdale grouse moor. Skiplam is spliced east to west by the Hodge Beck, which is born from a myriad of tinkling streams draining the high moor, and flows south through woodland and pasture beneath the commanding Sleightholmedale Lodge, whose owner loved her hunting and gardening in equal measure. The beck twists and turns through tight, green meadows here, but elsewhere its waters pummel tall cliffs of limestone and in places disappear into the bowels of the earth, only to re-emerge hundreds of yards lower down the valley.

The southern end of Skiplam is defined by the tiny Anglo-Saxon St Gregory's Minster, which dates from 1060 and has been described as the spiritual home of the Sinnington Hunt. I was destined to attend weddings and funerals here in almost equal measure over the years, and more than once have sounded the hunting horn's melancholy notes as the coffin of a long time supporter was carried from the church or lowered into a graveyard that is also the resting place of the writer Herbert Read, who was born and brought up at Muscoates Grange where I now live. If you know where to look, you can find the headstone marking his grave that displays the faded epitaph: 'Knight poet anarchist'. The distinguished graveyard is also the final resting place of former masters, Major Gordon Foster, Lord Westbury, and Thomas Parrington, who founded and judged the first Peterborough Hound Show in 1895. The intimate setting between quiet woodland, beck and sky is also the place where Rachel and I were married many years later, as well as being the venue for my final meet as a master of hounds.

Hounds could spend an entire day making Skiplam ring with their cry without ever leaving the valley, and when master in the 1970s, Lord Westbury liked to meet there every week in winter. However, with the division of the Feversham estate and the rise in popularity of shooting, Skiplam's days as a playground for hunting were numbered. The valley is now home to a well-established shoot, thankfully still accommodating hunting, but for many old-timers the release of common pheasants into this hallowed ground at the start of my second season was tantamount to sacrilege. Lady Clarissa and her husband, the charming and erudite bloodstock agent, Nico Collin, were determined that the two sports should coexist with as much harmony as possible, and the new gamekeeper was briefed accordingly. Walking around the Skiplam breeding earths the following spring, I marvelled how shoot advisors had identified a succession of sites chosen by generations of vixens for light, shelter and warmth as the best locations for their new release pens. Earths that had provided sanctuary to fox cubs for centuries were suddenly surrounded by 10ft-high wire and engulfed with swarms of cheeping poults.

Clarissa and Nico were true to their word, although I was unable to resist regular and persistent interventions on behalf of hunting that were largely borne with remarkable patience and understanding, however, on one occasion those virtues were tested to the full. I came across the neighbouring Farndale Hunt in full cry whilst collecting fallen stock in my Land Rover one March morning, and as they were streaming south through Skiplam, followed the hunt's progress until the fox was run to ground in a scar face close to Sleightholmedale Lodge. The dual protocols of leaving a fox that had been marked to ground in another hunt's country and not digging out in springtime applied, and having congratulated Mick Featherstone on the performance of his hounds, we all came away from the earth. I, however, resolved to return later, for I had become increasingly suspicious that the moorland keepers were wandering over their boundary to destroy foxes in forbidden territory.

The shadows were lengthening and herons croaking from their nests across the valley as I settled into the undergrowth to await the return of I knew not who – only with the strong hunch that someone would be back to set a box trap at the base of the cliff. Box traps are a particularly unpleasant tool of the moorland gamekeeper's trade that come into their own whenever solid rock makes it impossible to dig out a fox with shovel, pick or spade. The trap, which is no more than a 9-inch square wooden tunnel with bars at one end and a sliding door at the other, is wedged tight into one entrance of the earth, whilst the others are barricaded up with rocks. The prisoner inside has no option but to eventually emerge, and by scratching at the bars triggers the release of the trap door that seals his fate. Foxes have been known to resist crawling into such death traps for days, even weeks, when droplets of water inside a rocky den are available to sustain them, but there is an inevitability to the final outcome that must surely engender some remorse amongst even the hardest of perpetrators. I have never forgotten the words of one keeper describing a fox captured in this way. 'By the time I got him', he told me, 'the fox was light as a cork'.

Just as the valley began to fill with shade, an unseen vehicle could be heard pulling up on the far bank of the Hodge Beck, followed by hushed voices and the dull thud of doors quietly closed. Two figures weighed down with baggage emerged from the darkening trees, and hurried across a hundred yards of pasture to the rock earth beneath my vantage point. The men got to work quickly, one splashing diesel about the far entrance before filling it with stones, whilst his companion fitted a box trap into the other and started to make it good. In the current era of extensive buffer zones and thermal imaging it may seem quaint to imagine that the head keeper of a grouse moor could be so wrong-footed as Colin Short was that warm March evening more than twenty-five years ago, but he had been issued with clear instructions to confine his fox control to above the heather line and his apprehension was the culmination of a long-running battle between us. No one else involved in the ensuing and ultimately inconclusive saga felt half as passionately about the outcome as either Colin or I, but the lasting benefit was to have clipped his wings for the rest of my time in Yorkshire. Colin Short is no longer the head keeper of Bransdale, and we are the best of friends now, stopping to converse at hunt meets and on shoot days. 'You were only doing your job, and I was only doing mine,' is how the tall, dark man of brooding good looks recently described that distant springtime adventure.

The hunt Chairman, James Holt, presided over a third large shoot at his Ravenswick estate to the north of Kirkbymoorside, which occupied a valley only marginally smaller than Skiplam either side of the River Dove flowing south out of Farndale; a high, broad dale of neat drystone walls, small grass farms and, in spring, wild daffodils spread thick as yellow butter about the beck sides. In Stephen Todd, James had a true countryman as his head keeper, and someone old enough to recall the days when the Farndale Hunt was still a trencher-fed pack. The first time we met, Stephen greeted me with the news that a litter of nine cubs had been born in Faddell Rigg, and throughout my time at the Sinnington he could be guaranteed to provide accurate and genuine information as to where foxes were lying on the estate.

Stephen believed that every fox killed during winter resulted in two more coming to its funeral, and that it was pointless to remove foxes from a shoot if they were doing no harm. From him I learnt that foxes prefer plantations of certain age and tree type, and to factor in the wind and weather when planning a day's sport. Ravenswick became the preferred draw following the Boxing Day meet at Kirkbymoorside and I was once persuaded by Stephen to draw the Brickyards when it was really far too frozen to move off and hunt. There were three foxes at home, which had been lying together within five hundred yards of the meet, and although we had to pack up soon afterwards everyone was pleased to have enjoyed a hunt snatched from the elements. Four local packs of hounds came together for a joint meet on the Ravenswick estate to commemorate Stephen's retirement as head keeper in 2003, at which Willie Poole referred to him in his speech as 'King of gamekeepers, Prince of huntsmen and a very good friend'. He still follows hounds to this day.

James and Mary Holt were generous hosts at Ravenswick: a huge house with sweeping lawns, tennis court and swimming pool that for the last five years has stood empty and plundered of riches. I prefer to remember Ravenswick as the epicentre of hospitality and fun, a place of extravagant dinners, delicious wine and hunting guests from far and wide who were scooped up on a whim for dinner, bed and breakfast. We met there in winter too, usually in November, after which all comers would be invited back to hunting teas where home-cured bacon was washed down with tumblers of whiskey. Whenever the hunt needed to raise money in a hurry – such as to pay for the replacement of a broken bridge over the Costa Beck linking the Derwent and Sinnington Hunt countries – James and Mary would come to the rescue by staging a magnificent party that never failed to succeed.

James encouraged me to stalk the roe deer at Ravenswick, and even more generously allowed me to invite two or three farming guests to shoot whenever there was a boundary day on the estate. On these carefree days we covered the extensive boundaries of the shoot to gather a bag of up to a hundred head of game with guests taking it in turns to stand and beat. Being able to spend a day this way with farmers who enjoyed shooting was to foster good relations that in turn led to greater and easier access about the Sinnington Hunt country. There were so many other shooting invitations that I briefly became quite a good shot and, more importantly, learnt the many nuances of a sport that hunting ignores at its peril. Particularly enjoyable was an annual invitation to join the Nawton shoot in early December, where several of the guns also had some connection to the hunt. After the day ended, most of them headed straight for the bar at the Rose and Crown, where Wapper Woods would later carve half-inch-thick slabs of red beef from an enormous joint cooked to perfection by his wife. A regular haunt of earthstoppers, terriermen and shooters, to spend an hour at the crowded bar of this popular and sporting country pub was to glean a month's information on foxes, friends and foes of the hunt, much of it contradictory but all divulged with a peculiar blend of passion and subterfuge.

Apart from a handful of small rough shoots, shooting on the low side was confined to Nunnington estate, which by the happiest of coincidences fell under the management of Mary Clive, whose family own the estate, and her long-time boyfriend, Anthony Luke. Life for these two was an endless round of rearing, feeding, trapping and observing wildlife on an estate where foxes were always welcome, and their control very much left to the Sinnington Hunt. Luke and Mary's first love was fly fishing for salmon, and every May their car would be loaded up with spaniels, rods, reels and tackle for a three-week sojourn in Ireland. I was often asked to take care of the shoot whilst they were absent, which in reality meant little more at that time of year than trapping stoats, rats, squirrels, crows and magpies, and establishing the whereabouts of fox cubs that would be properly thinned out after we started hunting in September.

Despite my best endeavours, run-ins with shoots were inevitable from time to time, quite literally when hounds flew from Roppa moor to Easterside deep into Bilsdale Hunt country one high side Saturday, which resulted in a letter from the estate owner demanding the names of all involved in the mass trespass. His Lordship may have been a little surprised to read amongst the long list of names several of his friends and neighbours who had been following the hunt that day. A friendly meeting followed, after which the Sinnington hounds were permitted to run on to Hawnby if in pursuit of a fox, but only after 1 February. 'I cannot extend more favourable terms than those offered to our local hunt', wrote Lord Mexborough. On a happier occasion we met up with the Farndale at Fairycall Bridge after the hill pack had found a fox amongst the grouse and heather of Spaunton Moor and both packs combined to mark it to ground. A crescendo of wild holloas announced its departure a few minutes later, which left our hounds momentarily baffled, whereas the Farndale were quite used to such a din.

Shaun Mintoft was a young beat keeper on the neighbouring Duncombe Park estate, as keen on hounds, terriers and hunting as he was on shooting, but he was keener still on killing foxes by whatever means at his disposal, and not always within his shoot boundaries. We had to cancel hunting one day due to heavy snow, and not wanting to miss an opportunity to establish the whereabouts of high side foxes, I persuaded our amateur whipper-in and forester, John Cranage, to help me find an elusive artificial earth I knew Shaun had installed amongst windblow at the top of Ashdale. Contrary to saboteurs' allegations, artificial earths have nothing to do with bolstering the fox population, but have quite a role to play in its management. A carefully sited drain provides sanctuary for foxes in times of rough weather but is also a death trap from which they are easily extracted and killed. Somewhere at the top of Ashdale, John and I picked up two sets of fresh human footprints with the ominous feetings of a small dog beside and, by following them through the broken trees, soon arrived at the infamous drain. The flattened snow outside one entrance was infused pink with fresh blood, whilst two spent cartridges lying close by completed the story. I made sure that Shaun knew that I knew, and the speed with which this news reached him earned a respect that grew from that day onwards. In time, Shaun became a close ally of the hunt and a man I could turn to for accurate advice on where to find foxes.

I could not write of shooting and the Sinnington Hunt without reference to the remarkable Lupton brothers, who were busy burying some unidentifiable carcasses when I first called in to meet them one early summer afternoon in 1990. Former tenants of Newburgh estate, the family had purchased their own farm outright and delighted in running a small shoot there in defiance of their former landlords and the Newburgh keeper, who was never able to get the better of the countrymen's patient cunning. Appy and Fred lived under the same roof at Wass Grange as George and his wife, Ruby, surrounded by a chaotic jumble of farm buildings that were home to sheepdogs, spaniels, cattle, sheep, pigs and poultry according to the season of the year. The land directly in front of the house was given over to vegetable production, and although weeds and produce flourished in equal measure, George's beetroots, cabbages and onions were bigger and better than any I have ever come across.

A long, wooden building that had once served as the village hall was hidden around the back, and guests gathered in this dark and dusty room to munch their bait and sip hot tea from steel thermoses on shoot days. The hall had been bought following a Dutch auction with a neighbouring farmer in the 1950s, and then transported up to the farm in sections. The building has never seen a lick of paint since, and more than half a century of Yorkshire winters has exposed damp woodwork beneath once green paint. Inside the dusty shed, smelly chairs, dilapidated sofas, a grimy wooden table and several upturned boxes are surrounded by pigeon decoys, rolls of barbed wire, nuts, bolts, spanners, battered tins, fridges serving as cupboards, ancient farm implements and several live hens. A long metal pipe is suspended from the ceiling in the centre of the room from which game is hung by the neck using handcrafted wire holders, which over the years have saved the Luptons a small fortune in bailer twine. A pervading aroma of stale oil and rusting machinery seeps upwards from the thick concrete floor.

George was the most outgoing of the three brothers, and became a close friend, although I had to bite my tongue whenever he brought me up to date on his tally of foxes, which was impressive by anyone's standards for he was a complete artist with the snare. Before long, we were hunting across the Luptons' land, which hounds had not visited for decades but as the land lay beneath the crags, cliffs and forestry of Wass Moor, it was seldom without a fox. We went there for the first time on a September Monday but the fox in their field of kale made good his escape, much to the brothers' disappointment and anguish. I have been back many times since, sometimes with a pack of hounds, but often with gun, dog or net in pursuit of other Lupton game and vermin. I was asked by George to run my terrier through an earth in Crakyeland wood one spring, 'just to see if anything is there' and reluctantly agreed on the condition that George left his gun behind. Spooner rushed enthusiastically underground only to reappear a few minutes later hardly able to stand; George had forgotten that he had put a tub of sheep dip down the earth in order to deter potential tenants. Both my dog and our friendship survived.

I was invited to join the Luptons' shoot at least once a year; however, George always made it clear at the start of each day that foxes must not be shot if the MFH was a guest, a rule that was never broken until a day when I was unable to join the party until after the second drive. On arrival I checked with George that the guns had been briefed as usual, but he had forgotten to issue the warning. During the last drive before lunch someone gunned down a large dog fox close to Byland Abbey, which at once put me between a rock and a hard place. I thought of all those keepers who had been prevailed upon to leave foxes for the hunt and of the barside chat at the Rose and Crown that evening. I took the cartridges from my gun, thanked George for the day, and walked quickly from the shoot. I was not asked back to shoot pheasants at Wass Grange for more than a decade, although I spent many happy evenings waiting beside my friend for an autumn flight of duck. Appy, Fred and Ruby have all since passed away, but George endures into his nineties, still shooting straight and as bright-eyed and sharp as the day we first met. I visit him whenever time permits, and soak up the wit and wisdom of one of the finest countrymen it has been my privilege to know.

Above: The author as a child hunting on Flashman with his father Richard.

Left: The author's mother and father hunting with the Bedale, November 5th 1976.

Below: Stowe beagles kennel huntsman John "Nat" Thornton (on left) with the late Bill "Bossie" Boswell.

Left: Stowe beagles kill, 1980. From left:
The author, Frank Houghton-Brown,
the late Tom Bannister, Eddie Penrose,
Guy Hemsley, Andrew Neave, Johnny Portman,
James MacMillan. *(Jim Meads)*

Below: Stowe beagles in full cry from
Toddenham Manor meet, 1980. *(Jim Meads)*

Above: The author riding
Galaxy as lead horse in the
open class of the VWH team
chase at Kilkenny Farm, 1987.

Right: The author going down
to the start on Hung Dial the
day after becoming MFH on
May 2nd 1987.

Clockwise from top: First morning's hunting with the Spooners and West Dartmoor, August 11th 1987. From left to right: Tracy Doidge, the author, the late John Furze, Mike Doidge, Mary Anne Furze, unknown.

Spooners and West Dartmoor Carpenter '82 with Vixen Tor behind. Painted by Heather Budgett in 1988.

Spooners and West Dartmoor Demon '83 with Pew Tor behind. Painted by Heather Budgett in 1988.

Mary Anne Furze out hunting with Spooner in bag.

Above: The author crossing Huckworthy Bridge en route to his final meet as Spooners MFH on April 10th 1990. Mike Doidge and Jed Watson behind.

Left: BFSS Runners in the 1992 London Marathon. Left to right: The author, Marcus Armytage, Frank Houghton-Brown MFH, Martin Thornton, Robin Gundry MFH, Patrick Martin, Owen Inskip (organiser), Barry Todhun[...] Captain Ian Farquhar MF[...]

Above: Sinnington Gardiner '90 winner of the stallion hound class at Harrogate 1993 and saviour of a 16 mile hunt on January 22nd 1994.

Right: Desert Orchid out hunting with the Sinnington in retirement and ridden by Jeanie Brown, October 31st 1999.

Below: Former Ravenswick head keeper Stephen Todd with Rumsgill behind.

Right: Sinnington Elder '94 doghound champion at Harrogate 1997. *(Jim Meads)*

Below: Frank Houghton-Brown MFH (Middleton) with the bitch championship cup and the author with cups for champion doghound and most successful Yorkshire pack at Harrogate 1997. *(Jim Meads)*

Left: The author's last day hunting the Sinnington hounds from the meet at Douthwaite Dale on Waggie, March 25th 1998. *(Roy Parker)*

Left: Quorn bitches leaving the meet at Quenby Hall on Boxing Day, 1998.

Above: Quorn bitches breaking up a fox on Lowesby after a good hunt when Sinnington Beetle '97 caught the fox, January 29th 1999.

Below: An autumn hunting scene with the Quorn hounds near Gartree Hill, September 1999. Left to right: Neil Brooksbank (terrierman), David Bland (mounted, amateur whipper-in), the author MFH, Joss Hanbury MFH, Richard Mould (kennel huntsman and first whipper-in).

CHAPTER 9

Hounds, hunt staff and some great hunting runs

A new huntsman has many tasks, but getting to know each and every hound from the pack he has taken on is top of the list, closely followed by an accurate appraisal of their breeding. The MFHA has recently made hound pedigrees available online, but until then the only way of researching a hound's ancestry was to pore over copies of the *Foxhound Kennel Stud Book*, which dates from 1800 and in theory contains the breeding of every foxhound ever entered to hunting by a registered pack of hounds since that date. It is rare to find a full complement of stud books, however, Patrick Till tracked down a complete collection in east Yorkshire that I was able to purchase for the sum of £500, which took some finding at the time but remains one of the best investments I ever made.

The first step in getting to grips with breeding is to trace the tail female lines of every hound in kennel as far back as possible to a single foundation dam; in theory the fewer tail female lines that exist, the more uniform and level the pack will be in both looks and hunting ability. I discovered two principal female lines in the Sinnington kennels: the first and most dominant went back to Belvoir Susan 1867, which is often referred to as the 'old' Sinnington line, the second traced to a bitch called Puckeridge Actress, who was entered in 1888. The journey back to Actress took me via the Taunton Vale, which identified former master, Willie Poole, as having introduced a line that sparkles for its vitality, drive and enthusiasm to this day. Carefully bred packs are at risk of being spoilt when a new master or huntsman decides on a whim to breed from a variety of draft bitches without considering their pedigrees, or whether the introduction of a new female line is really necessary at all. With this in mind, I thought carefully before accepting Captain Ronnie Wallace's kind offer of three draft hounds from the Exmoor in Midnight '88, Tinkle '88 and Gaslight '89. Midnight went all the way back to Sir Thomas Mostyn's Lady 1801, Tinkle was fell bred on her dam's side but with a Peterborough champion as her sire, and Gaslight was descended from the celebrated Old Dominion Gorgeous '68, whom American Bill Brainard had given to Ronnie twenty-one years earlier.

Midnight proved to be not much more than a reliable worker, but Tinkle was without doubt the hardest-driving hound I have ever come across. Twice as fast as any hound in our kennel, she also operated on such a different mental plane that within weeks of her introduction my best hounds had forgotten to use their noses at a check, and instead looked about for Tinkle's willowy form racing over the horizon. There was no option but to draft the remarkable bitch, who combined a bloodhound's nose with the speed of a greyhound and was quite unsuited to any but the wildest of countries. She went to the Farndale, but comprehensively outclassed even those fell-bred, speedy hounds. However, Gaslight shone so brightly in her work that I incorporated her blood as a new female line at the Sinnington kennels and sent her back to Exmoor to be covered by a suitable doghound. The resultant litter distinguished themselves on their very first morning by continuing to own the line of a fox in Muscoates Whin some twenty minutes after it had been killed. One of those siblings, Grayling '84, was singled out for praise in my hunting diary when she recovered the line below Cherry Tree Farm two fields adrift from the rest of the pack during a fine two-and-a-half hour hunt in the snow on 4 January 1997. Another was identified as having cut out the work by Robin Smith-Ryland after hounds caught their fox halfway down Skiplam following a fast February hunt from Faddell Rigg.

I kept the hound breeding conventional to begin with, selecting good-looking stallion hounds who were also proven workers from the Exmoor, Middleton, Beaufort and VWH, in addition to using our own Gardiner '90, who was a son of the gift bitch, Duke of Beaufort's Radiant, and who had Blencathra Glider '76 for his grandfather. Gardiner covered a bitch from the old Puckeridge Actress line to produce a lovely litter that included Stonechat '93, a lively blue-mottle athlete who developed into a demon hunter. Four seasons into the job I began looking for a stallion hound to inject fresh blood into the Sinnington pack. By then I had become a firm fan of fell blood, first admired during visits to the Lake District as a schoolboy, which I had also seen work to good effect in the open Sinnington country.

The Border were showing fine sport at the time and I drove up to Northumberland for a day with Michael Hedley's pack of celebrated fox catchers, however, it was far too foggy at the meet to even unbox the hounds. Instead we retired into the warm farmhouse kitchen, and it wasn't until someone wiped the condensation from the windows that we realised the sun had come out and it was at last fit to hunt. On their huntsman's advice I selected Border Clasher '90 for the union with Stonechat. He was a little on the plain side but said to be a brilliant hunter with fell blood from the Blencathra, Eskdale & Ennerdale, Liddesdale and Melbreak coursing through his veins, much of it hitherto unused by any lowland pack. A few years later the grandson of that union came with me to Leicestershire and is down in the stud book as Quorn Bandit '98. The rangy, good-looking doghound became a fine hunter and the maternal grandfather of Zetland Woodcock '09, an influential sire who produced many good hounds for the Heythrop after he was sent to Chipping Norton towards the end of his career.

Exercising hounds every morning without having first cleaned and swilled out the yards seemed strange at first, but within a few weeks I had become accustomed to the new routine and Albert's cheery welcome as we explored quiet lanes on bicycles with my new pack. This included a few faithful friends from Dartmoor, and the broken-coated, amber eyed Fairy, an unentered hound of exceptional promise. I could also count on John Cranage for help in the hunting field, who has been a constant thread of continuity throughout the last quarter of a century of the Sinnington hunt's history. John whips in as an amateur to this day, whilst his son, Tom, made an outstanding success of hunting the Ampleforth beagles before promotion as first whipper-in to the Zetland. John has a dry sense of humour, is a prolific smoker of roll-ups with a voice to match, and has the ability to get well on point and read the progress of any hunt. During my early seasons the terrier work was shared by livestock haulier and Harome man, Jim Dodsworth, and Steven Wilson from Liverton Mines across the moor; Jim did the navigation and Steven worked his terriers.

If I had any lingering doubts about a move north, they were dispelled during the first morning's hunting in Muscoates Whin. As hounds hurried through a strip of artichokes on their way to covert, they put up and caught a fox at the feet of Hugh Murray Wells before a morning of continuous hunting, during which three separate coverts all held several foxes. It was obvious that I had inherited a good pack of hounds from my predecessor, Alastair Stewart, a quiet and effective huntsman who rode straight as a die and disdained anything as modern as a hunt jump. Badger '84 was one of the best: a large, seventh season, broken-coated dog of Welsh descent, who together with his little sister, Beetle, was as honest as the day is long.

The first season was characterised by a plethora of foxes and busy days, including a fine ninety-minute, 11-mile hunt from Pockley in December, but we had to wait until February before achieving the elusive four-mile point. The following season the high side went one better by producing an 18-mile run from Gillamoor in November, and Muscoates Whin was already earning a special place in my affections by providing a December fox that we hunted for 15 miles and two-and-a-half hours before he saved his brush by running through electric fencing below Great Edstone. Eight weeks later a fox from Major Shaw's Bowforth covert made a five-mile point to the east of Great Barugh.

The arrival of Richard Mould from the Haydon as first whipper-in and kennel huntsman for the start of my third season coincided with a run of fine sport that endured for the rest of our time in Yorkshire. My hunting diaries from those years describe some remarkable runs, the likes of which are unlikely to be seen again. Although we enjoyed a six-mile point across the vale from South Ings below Kirkbymoorside to Nelson Gate above Helmsley, the most exceptional hunts were the domain of the wilder high side north of the A170, where three especially memorable runs took place. The fog was so bad at Hutton-le-Hole on 8 January 1994 that the meet was delayed until 12 noon, much to the disappointment of Patrick Till, who decided not to hunt that day at all. Hounds moved off in poor visibility and at first struggled on an even poorer scent in the moorside wilderness that is Faddell Rigg, but the fog lifted as they approached Stoneley Woods and scent dramatically improved. We had to gallop hard to keep in touch as the pack scaled steep Rollgate bank half a mile ahead of us, and continued at top pace out on to the moor at Bonfield Ghyll. Mains electric here stung hounds and threatened to shut down the hunt, which was saved by little Tynedale Mayfly '91, who Richard had brought with him from the Haydon.

The rest of the pack flew to her cry beyond the hateful wire fence and the hunt continued through the forestry at East Moors into Cowhouse Bank and on to Baxton's Wood above Helmsley. Here, with every forestry track frozen like glass and tall drifts of snow on the verges, horses were sent home after a gruelling two-and-a-quarter-hour hunt, including the mount of Fred Collin, across whose Nawton Tower estate much of the run had taken place. We transferred to Land Rovers and caught up with the pack above Carlton at dusk, which is more than six miles in a straight line from the find, but I lay awake that night wondering whether hounds might have caught their fox had it not been for the delay at Bonfield Ghyll.

We went one better two weeks later following Rosanna James' meet at Sleightholmedale Lodge on a fox found in the bracken beds close to Cherry Tree Farm. Hounds ran steadily north into wild moorland, crossing the Bransdale road below Ousegill Bridge and hunting past the Countess's home at Bransdale Lodge, deep into Farndale Hunt country. Having scored a six-and-a-half mile point, the fox must have been headed by a hill walker here for he swung back sharply to the east, causing the only serious check of a 16-mile hunt. High up amongst the wind-lashed heather, this was Gardiner's finest hour, for the handsome, mottled son of Radiant with a smattering of fell blood from his sire, Cotswold Glencoyne '85, cast downwind and recovered the line. Ten minutes later he keeled over with an apparent heart attack, only to regain composure and resume his place at the head of affairs as hounds poured off the moor into Farndale above Spout House.

Even twenty years ago it was remarkable to have run for 16 miles across North Yorkshire without encountering a shooting party, but our luck finally gave out when our tired pilot ran into an afternoon drive of the Farndale shoot. Thankfully, the keeper, Frank Croft, was a firm friend of hunting and a sound ally of his local Farndale pack, but the hunt ended in confusion and we plodded wearily home without a brush for our efforts. Years later Frank divulged that hounds had overhauled their quarry on the banks of the River Dove, but he never explained why I had to wait so long for this welcome news. The sporting artist, Robin Furness, happened to be following in a car that day and saw Gardiner leading the pack at Ousegill Bridge. His painting of that scene now hangs above my bed, a reminder of a great run, an even greater hound, and of Waggie too, my game mare from Dartmoor who had carried me so well throughout the longest hunt she ever knew.

There was no such confusion at the end of the third great hill hunt of that era, which got under way at 12.30 p.m. from the north-west corner of Pinderdale in December 1996. The fox must have slipped away before any of the points, for no one saw him leave, only hounds flying across the big grass enclosures to sink Newgate Bank and head out across moorland so bleak and wild that Peter Teasdale once lost a horse up there for three whole days. The field were hopelessly adrift by the time hounds reached Ankness, 5 miles into what was destined to be a hunt of nearly 20 miles. Fog had settled on to the high ground beyond, but Richard and I were able to keep in touch thanks to helpful information from hill walkers, who indicated the hunt's progress steadily north for several miles along Shaw Ridge.

Having made an 8 mile point, our fox turned short of the disused line at Blowforth crossing, beyond which lies Baysdale Moor and the headwaters of the River Esk, which flows into the North Sea at Whitby. A mile to the east we emerged from the fog to look down onto the pristine, green landscape of Farndale with hounds racing like a string of distant pearls alongside the infant River Dove. Smoke from scattered farmsteads furled lazily into blue skies above a landscape that seemed devoid of human life; only a tinkle faint as beck water betrayed the presence in the dale of a pack in full cry. We watched them from our vantage point on tired horses, as alone and unassisted they overcame sheep foil, pig netting and tarmac to run into their fox at Hollins Farm and conclude a fast and brilliant two-hour run.

Such hill hunts were exceptional for including long points within the distance hounds actually ran, but there were many others of more than 10 miles that did not comprise a point worth mentioning – which I was brought up to understand is anything less than 4 miles in a straight line. Being better foxed and easily accessible, the vale produced more consistent sport than the heavily shot high country, where it tended to be either feast or famine. Although I survived eight seasons at the Sinnington without experiencing a completely blank day, there were a few close calls, and more days than I care to remember with just one fox afoot. However, whenever conditions were right, good vale days came thick and fast and my diaries are full of references to points of 4 and 5 miles, and exhilarating days when we covered most of the vale between Harome in the west and Habton in the east.

On 10 January 1995 hounds scored two 4 mile points in a day, the first from Habton Whin, the second on a fox that jumped up like a hare from a wheat field below Great Barugh and was marked to ground 11 miles later in the dark a few fields short of Pickering. During my last season we had a fine six-and-a-half mile point from a stack of straw bales near Brawby, during which hounds swam the Rivers Rye and Dove to run through Habton Whin and enter the Derwent country below Kirby Misperton. They swung south here to scorch across the lonely, arable plains beside the Costa Beck and swim the Rye for a second time into Middleton country and, with a brace in front, marked both foxes to ground within a field of the Malton to Pickering road at Eden Camp. Vale foxes under pressure sometimes crossed the main A170 to seek refuge in the hills before going on to produce long hunts, but during an 11 mile run one March our hunted fox recrossed the main road for a second time to end up back at West Ings in the vale.

Another great vale hunt took place following a meet at Sunley Hill on 28 February 1996 that had been put back to noon on account of a hard frost. After a busy morning, hounds were taken to draw Richardson's Plantation at 3 p.m., which was just beginning to look like holding foxes again having been clear felled and replanted a few years earlier. The deep, booming voice of Middleton Stalwart '90 confirmed a fox at home, which ran eastwards across old turf to cross the Ness lane with hounds in close attendance, continuing over the Tates' farm to swim the Dove by Sparrow Hall. The fox had established a useful lead by the time the hunt reached Normanby Strip, which in those days was under the benign control of Philip Bell but is now a tortuous tangle of mains electric that the owner refuses to switch off.

Having made his furthest point, the fox swung back through the hunt covert of Rookbarugh, which is the subject of a famous Lionel Edwards painting, prints of which grace the walls of many hunting households in this corner of Yorkshire. I lifted hounds to a view over the Great Edstone road beyond this thick thorn covert, but that was the only time they were touched during an extraordinarily long, and at times rather slow, three-and-a-half hour hunt. The pack hunted vociferously and beautifully through successive fields of sheep as perfectly tuned into the line as I have ever seen; not the breathtaking, blistering pace of a breast-high flyer, but the steady and faultless progress that is the hallmark of a genuine holding scent. The longest hunts are invariably achieved under such conditions, but at this stage it seemed unlikely that hounds would ever catch their quarry, yet to lose him seemed equally improbable.

Our horses were all done by the time we reached Alan Lockwood's smallholding at Brawby much later, with my horn lost in a ditch somewhere along the way; however, the puppy walker came to the rescue by offering his own horn from the mantelpiece and his stables for tired horses. We jumped on to the bonnet of John King's Land Rover and, on catching up with the action, saw that hounds had finally reduced their pilot's lead. They fairly flew down the banks of the River Severn before coursing him back to Flint Hall, where he was killed in the gloaming after a 17 mile hunt.

Much credit for the performance of the Sinnington hounds during the 1990s must go to Richard Mould, who was a dedicated, loyal and brilliant combination of kennel huntsman and first whipper-in. Richard's quiet and discreet manner on the hunting field had an immediate impact on hounds, whose hunting got better and better as their confidence grew. Richard and his wife, Debbie, made an excellent team, and in the eight years we worked together I cannot recall a cross word with a man who was always receptive to a new or different approach to any of hunting's numerous challenges. Richard's dedication in kennels was evidenced by the long hours he spent after a morning's autumn hunting, checking every pad of every hound that had been out that day; to visit the kennels on a September afternoon was to be presented with a saucer full of lethal blackthorns that had been extracted before the poison could set in. In a dry autumn when the clay floor of hunt coverts was harder than a hound's pad, thorns could be particularly troublesome. Despite Richard's best endeavours there was always a hound or two that ended up missing most of the season due to a thorn injury sustained in the autumn.

Halfway through my time at the Sinnington I was approached by Richard and Penny Tyacke, who were joint masters of the Atherstone in Warwickshire, to see whether we had an opening for their eighteen-year-old son, also called Richard, to join the team as an amateur whipper-in. Michael and Claire Brown agreed to take the unknown young man on as a lodger, although I thought his parents would run a mile having met Michael for the first time one Sunday morning. The four of us arrived at the Browns' house in Wombleton at 11 a.m. to find the curtains drawn, music blaring and a pervading stench of alcohol and tobacco. Michael eventually stumbled shirtless down the stairs whilst buckling up his belt above a bulging white stomach. If the Tyackes, immaculately attired in their Sunday best, thought the lodgings a little unsuitable, they said nothing, and the Browns' home turned out to be perfect digs in every respect.

With Richard as kennel huntsman and a loyal retainer called Dick, Michael Brown decided from the start that the new lodger would have to go by a different title and christened him Junior, a name that stuck for the rest of his time in Yorkshire. Richard has his own stories of his season at the Sinnington, including one about being asked to block a hole with his brand-new Patey hat, but I remember him as a valuable addition to the team, as single-minded about hunting as the rest of us, and a fine horseman to boot. When Junior's own horses went lame, Michael provided a succession of others for him to ride, including a green one that required a lot of stitches after following me from concrete to concrete over an upright iron gate in a farmyard near Cropton. Far from being cross, Michael only smiled and announced that the horse concerned had gone up £1,000 in value. Now seldom referred to as Junior, Richard Tyacke is currently showing fine sport with Sir Watkin Williams-Wynn's (Wynnstay) fabled hunt as one of the top amateur huntsman in the country. During his 1994–95 season at the Sinnington we accounted for a record 39½ brace of foxes, 29 brace of them caught on top.

It was not all good of course. There were plenty of frustrations, mistakes and disappointments along the way and a few regrets too. One of these was buying a high-class rangy machine of a horse from a local dealer at the start of my first season. Elmo was far from straightforward but Terry Wharton had designed a special bit that suited the bay gelding so well that he went as my second horse to Garrowby when the Middleton hounds were sidelined with the cough. All went swimmingly until I foolishly asked him for an impossible leap coming away from Baffam and we ended up on the rim of a deep, wide gutter with a slipped bridle and a broken bit. Elmo was never the same from that moment on, and that was the last time I asked any horse to take on an unjumpable fence.

Elmo also had an unhappy role in what was possibly the worst day's hunting I ever had. The spring day started inauspiciously with hounds catching a three-legged fox on Brink Hill, but got far worse when Elmo dropped dead beneath me of a heart attack at the top of Sutton Bank, where we were surrounded by bemused sightseers. Meanwhile, Dick Scott, a kindly council worker from Harome in whose house I have enjoyed many a Sunday lunch, was driving the hunt lorry carrying second horses beneath the archway that spans the road at Byland Abbey, which would have been fine had the hunt lorry not been taller than the beautiful stone monument. Dick also helped with the earth stopping and on another occasion I met him driving away from the rock earths at Cockerill Tip as hounds raced towards them at the end of a fast evening run. 'Don't worry, sir', he shouted as I galloped past, 'I've unblocked the holes'.

That the fox found refuge was especially frustrating as we had most unusually drawn a blank until nearly 3 p.m., and then found a leash all together in a pile of stones close to the kennel. Hounds had settled at once on a burning scent with only me, Richard, Andrew Osborne and Owen Inskip visiting from the Beaufort in attendance. Andrew had a bad fall over a gate and broke his collarbone; we rather unkindly galloped on, for to stop and assist would have been to lose the hounds. The following week I invited Andrew around to Primrose Cottage for a drink and asked him to join me in the mastership, which much reduced the workload for my final two seasons. Andrew maintains that he expected to be invited to wear the hunt buttons that evening, but he took to his new role like a duck to water and in the Cottesmore now hunts one of the great amateur packs of the country. It was entirely fitting that we caught a fox in the Osborne's farmyard at Low Northolme when Barney White-Spunner came to write us up for *The Field* the following season.

Well organised earth stopping and keeping foxes above ground played a significant role in the run of good sport, as did the use of fieldcraft and attention to detail. We headed south into the vale after one Boxing Day meet because I had been told that foxes were working an old rubbish tip at the edge of the Kirkbymoorside industrial estate. A few days beforehand I walked the full length of the rabbit-proof fence that divides the south side of the tip from arable farmland and found 6 inches of top wire stained brown where a fox had regularly been jumping in and out of his hiding place, and his feetings in the soft ground beneath. John Cranage left the meet well ahead of hounds to take up station on point, and as we rode out of the market square Jim Dodsworth and his helpers started to beat out half an acre of rubbish and rusty cars. The fox came away moments before I arrived, hounds were laid on, and we ran four miles straight across the vale to a hedgerow near Muscoates, where the fox had climbed up a tree.

For obvious reasons I never saw that particular fox again, but there were others I came to know well on account of the line taken when hunted or by some distinguishing physical feature. I first met the bob-tailed Sinnington fox when drawing Bill Baldwin's tiny coverts south of the A170 in September 1994, but he had little difficulty beating us to the Marton Head earths that day. A month later we found him again, this time in the high country half a mile to the north at Bishops Hagg, and with the help of Belfry '90, Darling '91 and Ernest '94 succeeded in marking him to ground in an open badger sett on the banks of the River Seven. He was seen again in December leaving Dawson Wood, although we were hunting another fox at the time, and he did not reappear until Patrick Till holloared him away from the very same covert eleven months later. Patrick's wife, Bridget, viewed my bob-tailed friend away from Howlgate Head on the last day of the season and hounds marked at the Dawson Wood drain after a short spin. I was somewhat surprised – and secretly relieved – when we bolted and caught a fox with a very long brush twenty minutes later.

Tange Pickard watched our fox disappear down a badger sett behind Appleton-le-Moors the following October, but that was destined to be our last encounter with a fox that had featured seven times in three years. By a remarkable coincidence, I found the bob-tailed fox dead on the edge of Howlgate Head whilst walking country a few months later, and felt a pang of real sorrow for his departure. I had seen him myself just once during that September morning on the edge of the vale, and he had never provided a good hunt. But for me the bob-tailed fox had become a beacon of hope for all high side foxes, for to survive in that country for three long years was a truly remarkable achievement.

CHAPTER 10

Hunting and conservation at the Sinnington

The hunting season in Yorkshire drew to a natural close during March, but there was important work to be done in the hunt coverts long before the thorn came into bud. Minutes from early Sinnington Hunt committee meetings reveal that cutting down blackthorn coverts such as Muscoates Whin after the thorns had grown tall and cold was one the single biggest items of expenditure. Huge bonfires were built from the hand cut thorns, and by the following autumn suckers had recolonised the bare ground with thick warm cover, a benefit that lasted for at least fifteen years, after which the cycle would begin again.

Over the last century much of the blackthorn in the Sinnington Hunt coverts has been replaced by naturally seeded hawthorn, which can be laid horizontally on to the ground where it continues to flourish. Laying hawthorn lets in light, which encourages a proliferation of undergrowth that provides near-perfect habitat for a diverse range of wildlife, especially songbirds such as chaffinches, warblers and buntings. Blackthorn ultimately dies after being laid, but there are many hunt conservationists either unaware of this fact or unable to tell the difference between two very different thorns, one of which is easy to manage, the other difficult and time-consuming. Equally frustrating are well-meaning supporters who decide to create a covert on their own initiative but end up planting neat rows of deciduous trees that grow up to deprive the woodland floor of life-sustaining light. In almost every case, much better habitat would have been achieved by simply fencing the area off and leaving nature to her work.

A working party of half a dozen fit men with chainsaws and gardening gloves can transform an area of barren hawthorn into a fox-holding covert in a single afternoon, and there were always volunteers to help with covert laying on Sunday mornings in February, or if hunting was cancelled due to frost. Mr Bulmer from Sleights Farm near Amotherby kindly gave me permission to fence off a stand of twenty or thirty tall hawthorns that stood close by a deep gutter. A few of us dropped the thorns one February afternoon, leaving the tallest tree until last, which had a large squirrel drey in its upper branches. When the thorn was eventually cut and pulled down, a squirrel shot out of his home and disappeared amongst the newly created scrub. Despite its tiny area, Squirrel Wood became one of the most reliable of all the hunt coverts, and living testament to what can be achieved with just a few hours' work.

The benefits of covert laying to all kinds of wildlife, flora and fauna, were so indisputable that I decided on a whim to apply to the local, Liberal-led, Ryedale District Council for a grant to tackle this work combined with some replanting in certain hunt coverts. Other landowners were being assisted in their conservation projects, so it seemed entirely fair that the Sinnington Hunt should enjoy the same support as everyone else, and be considered solely on the merits of our proposal. Somewhat to my surprise, an award of £400 was agreed by the Community Services Committee in October 1994, which whipped up such a furore of protest from the League Against Cruel Sports (LACS) that the grant was amended at the subsequent meeting of the full council to the offer of expert advice and assistance by the Countryside Managements Officer.

The vote was split straight down the middle, with fifteen councillors voting for and fifteen against financial assistance being offered to the hunt, but what I found most galling was listening to the committee Chairman, misquoting from an article that had recently been published in the Saturday *Telegraph Magazine*.

Johnny Beardsall had reported that I was paid a guarantee of £35,000 with which to run the hunt, but this fact was presented to the council as if it were a personal salary and not a sum that had to provide a living for three members of hunt staff and much more besides. I sometimes wonder whether the vote would have been different had I stood up and objected at that moment, but it was clear that any intervention from the public gallery would not be tolerated so I had no choice but to bite my lip and suffer in silence.

That the hunt ended up without financial assistance was by then academic, for we had been awarded a grant, even though it was worthless. The grant application generated huge interest in the press and other media, nearly all of it positive. The *Daily Telegraph* quoted the LACS as condemning the application as a 'clever piece of public relations', which unwittingly turned out to be true despite my original intentions. I was interviewed on Radio 4's *Today* programme, and several years later was astonished to be told by a farming friend in Kenya that he had listened to the programme whilst driving his tractor in Laikipia. The media interest in hunting resulted in the local *Malton Gazette* inviting readers to write in with their own views on the subject, which resulted in such a deluge of overwhelmingly positive correspondence that the paper agreed to publish a five hundred-word report in the sports pages from each of the three Ryedale hunts every week throughout the following season. This led to accusations in print from Ryedale's most prominent objector to hunting, Tom Woodward, that the paper was run for the benefit of foxhunting in general and myself in particular.

Mr Woodward has been a thorn in the side of Ryedale Hunts for nearly three decades, but I am not aware that he has ever caused any serious damage and there have been spells lasting for years when he has completely disappeared off the radar. Hunt saboteurs were a brief problem in the 1990s, which the principal Ryedale hunts addressed in response to North Yorkshire Police advice by employing stewards under the direction of a former military man to prevent trespass and disruption of a lawful activity, although we could not afford this level of protection during autumn hunting in September and October. Sometimes Mr Woodward and his cronies would stake out the kennel drive in the dark and follow the hunt lorry to wherever we were hunting early that morning, which the hunt staff understandably found intimidating and unreasonable.

After one such escapade it seemed only fair to give the other side a taste of their own medicine, which meant that the terrierman and his pals from Liverton Mines ended up following Tom and Debbie Woodward going about their lawful business once they had finished trying to disrupt ours. To our men's surprise, the car they were following turned left at Pickering towards Whitby, then pulled up beside roadside stables. This was too much for our team, who wound down the window and shouted 'Shergar' as they drove slowly past. I had the police on the telephone within the hour, but they appeared sympathetic once I explained that the veiled reference to horse abduction was nothing more than the sort of joke we had been enduring for months. Many years later, and in a different life, I enrolled for evening classes in Spanish and discovered that the attractive woman in my small group of fellow students at Pickering was none other than Debbie Woodward. As we walked out of the building, following the first of several tutorials together, Debbie introduced me to her son, and the relationship between us for the rest of the course was entirely cordial.

In June 1994 I submitted Hutton Common as the Sinnington's entry for an inter-hunt conservation competition run by the MFHA. The steep gorse bank was nearly four hectares in size and a favourite haunt of Ravenswick foxes on account of the site being kept warm and thick by Stephen Todd's policy of burning a small area of grown-out gorse each spring. This strategy also allowed violets to flourish alongside thick tendrils of very young gorse, which created an ideal habitat for the complicated life cycle of the pearl-bordered fritillary butterfly. The treasurer of Butterfly Conservation wrote to congratulate the management on achieving 'what the eastern half of England has failed to do' and pointed out that Hutton Common was home to Yorkshire's only surviving colony of these rare and beautiful butterflies. The project was particularly close to my heart, for I had been a keen lepidopterist as a schoolboy, and although the Heythrop won the competition outright, the efforts of the Ravenswick head keeper gained us the coveted regional award for the North and an invitation to lunch at the Berkeley hotel in London. Sadly, there have been no similar initiatives since, and the many benefits that hunting brings to conservation have never been less championed than during the current post-ban era.

There has always been a small covert at the bottom of the long grass field that goes with the Sinnington kennels at Nawton, with a similar-sized block of rough pasture beside. It seemed obvious on the basis of symmetry alone to plant up the adjacent grassland, so this time I applied to the North Yorkshire County Council for grant aid in establishing new woodland. Paul Jackson, the North Yorkshire Rural Conservation Officer, wrote to me in April 1996 to advise that the grant had been approved and the payment would be with us shortly. We were able to create a wood that was almost exclusively hawthorn, which was subsequently laid after the trees had grown to a reasonable height and is now as warm and thick as any covert in the land. As this grant was not discretionary or subject to debate, the creation of new woodland by a hunt in Ryedale attracted no publicity at all, in contrast to a well-orchestrated campaign to have the popular grey steeplechaser, Desert Orchid, photographed out hunting with the Sinnington in October 1996. A photograph of 'Dessie', ridden by Jeannie Brown and surrounded by hounds duly appeared in the *Daily Telegraph*, alongside a story explaining the valuable role hunting can offer retired racehorses.

My interest in covert management and conservation led in 1996 to an invitation from the Duke of Northumberland to join a new British Field Sports Society (BFSS) Conservation Committee that he had agreed to chair. Attending meetings at Syon House in London alongside such luminaries as David Bellamy, Will Garfit and the BFSS Chief Executive, Robin Hanbury-Tenison, was an opportunity to broaden my conservation horizons and ensure that hunting's contribution to conservation was not overlooked, however, despite the Committee's best intentions it eventually ran out of steam and became incorporated into the Badminton Conservation Trust, which over the years was able to safeguard several woodlands for the benefit of both hunting and conservation. My contribution these days is limited to looking after Muscoates Whin for the hunt, but I make sure that the rides are always cut out in summer, lay thorn when necessary, and ensure that the covert is left quiet and undisturbed. Occasionally I wander down the green ride in mid-summer just to admire the vigour and vitality of an ecosystem that is home to an astonishing variety of birds and wildlife.

CHAPTER 11

Summers at the Sinnington

The achievement of long hunting runs is not just about excellent staff and a pack of hounds carefully bred and well handled; it's also the product of a good relationship with the farmers and landowners. With this in mind I decided to continue to collect the fallen stock at the Sinnington just as I had done on Dartmoor, although skinning and associated perks became the domain of my kennel huntsman. In this way frequent and regular contact was maintained with nearly all of our farming hosts, and it was rare to complete the daily flesh round without also walking some country or calling in on other local people that might be affected by our activities in their area. These included an expanding number of horse and pony owners, who often rented a field or two on the edge of a village and who much appreciated being notified when hounds were likely to be in the vicinity. The modern trend is for masters to personally visit most, if not all, the farmers whose land they hope to cross when out hunting in a few days' time, but this approach cannot work for a hunt that is regularly producing points of more than four miles, especially when there is no clue as to which direction the hunted fox might run. In 1990 a fox found just about anywhere in the Sinnington country could set sail on any bearing without impediment, for there was not a single railway line, dual carriageway, hospital, cash machine or supermarket in the entire four hundred square miles we hunted across, and only one comparatively quiet main road. Furthermore, most of the shoots were generous enough to allow us to run in if in pursuit of a fox, although drawing was a different matter altogether.

The Sinnington country remains unspoilt and rural to this day; we now have a few cash machines but many other trappings of modernisation are still refreshingly absent. I remembered the acute frustration whenever the beagles at Stowe 'ran out of the draw' and had to be stopped, and was determined to do everything possible to ensure that we could achieve long hunts without upset or problems. The solution was to send meet cards out twice a season to every single farmer, paddock owner, gamekeeper and landowner in the country, with the dates on which we were likely to be in their area underlined, together with a letter pleading forbearance in the event of a long hunt. This approach was consolidated by regular visits incorporated into the flesh round, during which I was able to ascertain whether a carding system was acceptable or not; some farmers were happy with my proposal, others asked for a telephone call, and a few insisted on a visit. As I devoted almost as much time on reconnaissance as on actual hunting, plenty of visiting always took place, and in time it became clear who were pleased to see the MFH and who preferred to be left in peace; but it was rare for there to be any fallout or unpleasantness after hounds scored a long hunt and ran out of the draw.

The summer months were an opportunity to take the foot off a pedal that had been flat to the boards for the previous seven months, although I did complete the London Marathon to raise funds for the BFSS in 1992 alongside Ian Farquhar, Frank Houghton-Brown, Barry Todhunter, Martin Thornton, Patrick Martin and Marcus Armytage. I also walked many miles during the second half of April and early May each year searching for litters of cubs in order to build up an idea of the fox population throughout the area we hunted, for the role of a well-organised hunt is to manage rather than simply control foxes like common vermin. There is a narrow window of opportunity in early May that coincides with young rooks leaving their nests when it is easy to identify the whereabouts of litters by the trampled grass, fur and feathers surrounding an occupied earth. In time I became adept at spotting revealing brown smudges of exposed soil or blanket-sized tracts of worn grass amongst an otherwise green hedge back. By the middle of the month the corn and undergrowth have grown up to such an extent that foxes forsake their homes underground and spend the rest of the summer on top.

The first Tuesday of June was a time to get scrubbed up for a rare visit to London and attend the MFHA AGM at Hyde Park Barracks, which was traditionally held the day before the Epsom Derby. Captain Charles Barclay used to organise a private luncheon for favoured masters at the Cavalry and Guards Club in Piccadilly, which I was invited to attend having completed my fourth season as an MFH. Robin Smith-Ryland insisted that Frank and I accompany him to White's Club in St James's for a drink beforehand, during which we greedily devoured a bowl of gulls' eggs left out on the bar. It was only when we came to leave that I realised the barman had been keeping a tally of each egg consumed for addition to the bill of our generous host.

A few years later Willie Wakeham joined the Hon. Bobby Corbett in the Eglington mastership, which was cue for the red-faced, stuttering but magnanimously generous Bobby to host his own pre-AGM lunch at Wiltons for Willie and his amateur huntsman friends. An invitation was also extended to the more glamorous wives of senior masters. Bobby picked up the tab and we dined on fresh lobster; I'm afraid I did not take much persuading to jump ship and join my friends at Wiltons. After Bobby died, Libby Beckett and Sarah Davidson kindly hosted the lunch for one more year, but we all agreed it was just not the same without the man who used to catch the bus from his Scottish home dressed in full hunting regalia. Bobby's memory lives on at the Great Yorkshire Show each year where a cup for the best brood bitch at the hound show is presented in his memory. There are few masters of hounds these days likely to have a runner in the Derby, and when Lord Daresbury succeeded Michael Richardson as Chairman, he most democratically moved the meeting to the more central location of his Belfry Hotel near Birmingham. This was a regrettable change of scenery for young MFHs looking forward to visiting the bright lights of London, but for everyone else the change made sense. Later, the venue was moved again to Cheltenham racecourse, but neither place held the same cachet as London, nor could a racecourse lunch compete with the fabulous fresh seafood at Wiltons.

June also signalled the start of the puppy show seasons; as well as organising our own show in July there were judging obligations to fulfil the length and breadth of Britain, which sometimes included one of the five major regional hound shows. For a few lively years, high summer was also marked by Mary Holt's 'Not the Pony Club Camp' at Ravenswick, where the lucky participants were forbidden to clean tack, groom horses or engage in any other of the more mundane aspects of pony management. Instead, they were taken to Sandsend to gallop on the beach at low tide, taught how to shoot rabbits, poach trout and catch a piglet doused in slippery oil. James Holt and I were roped in to take the children lamping rabbits one night, which we did with a small-bore shotgun and a four-wheel-drive vehicle with two sunroofs; the children stood up on the passenger seats and took aim through the rear one above their heads. An hour into this activity, the sunroof above the driver's seat shattered as Tom Holt pulled the trigger on another bunny, while at the same time James slumped forward over the steering wheel like a dead man. Even in those days James was heavier than average, and my first thought was how we could remove him in order to get home. Moments later I saw his fingers moving amongst hair filled with shattered glass and realised that the front sunroof had disintegrated when Tom had used it to rest the gun on and fire. No one was hurt, but we drove straight home in stony silence, pondering what might have been.

Mary invited the mothers and other ladies to tea in the hunt marquee one afternoon each camp, after which Michael Brown and I judged the competition for the best set of ankles. The ladies lined up inside the tent, at which point the canvas was rolled up just far enough for us to inspect the ankles on show, but not sufficiently high to see the rest of the body to which they belonged. After much deliberation that included plenty of feeling and prodding, we selected an exquisite pair of ankles as the winner. The wall of the tent was rolled up slowly and fully to reveal as the winner an elegant but elderly, grey-haired lady amongst a crowd of much younger glamorous mummies.

York race week in August was a perfect opportunity to invite racegoers from all over the country to join us at a lavish Ebor Ball, which Laura Collin enthusiastically and skilfully revived to such a degree that it became for many an unmissable part of the racing calendar. Held at venues that included the spectacular terraces at Rievaulx, the event became a significant contributor to Sinnington Hunt funds, but ran out of steam after its organiser met and married the master and huntsman of the Meynell and South Staffordshire in Derbyshire. At the other end of the scale were village dances masquerading as hunt balls where farmers' wives put on huge spreads of food and a discotheque provided the music. A handful of guests wore full evening dress on these occasions, but most turned up in suits determined to enjoy the evening to the full, especially the one held at Pockley village hall in February when game keepers celebrated the end of the shooting season and things often got a little rough in the small hours. The image of a handsome fox that adorned Pockley village hall has been replaced by a collie dog and sheep, and the wondrous hunt balls of Habton, Helmsley, Kirkbymoorside and Pockley have long since faded into obscurity.

During my last summer at the Sinnington the newly formed Countryside Alliance organised a huge rally in Hyde Park in response to the Labour MP for Worcestershire's private member's bill to ban hunting with dogs, which was given its first reading on 17 June 1997. Worcestershire huntsman, Julian Barnfield, had famously declined to shake the hand of a man determined to destroy his way of life and livelihood when Michael Foster paid a token visit to the Worcestershire Hunt kennels and later said of the MP: 'He didn't care a jot about any of us, or the consequences of a ban – he said shooting foxes was the answer, but when we showed him a rifle bullet he didn't know what it was.'

Mark Miller Mundy's inspired idea of the rally being publicised by the arrival of walkers setting off from far-flung corners of England and Scotland quickly gathered momentum, and a dedicated office was established by Charles and Chips Mann at their Gloucestershire home. During June core walkers left Coldstream in the Scottish borders, Caldbeck in the Lake District, Plas Machynlleth in Wales, and Madron in Cornwall with the intention of converging at Hyde Park in time for the 10 July rally. The dedicated volunteers who walked the entire way to Hyde Park were accompanied on a daily basis by varying numbers of supporters unable to undertake the complete journey. I met the Welsh marchers gathered outside the town hall at Plas Machynlleth on 27 June at the start of their long walk beneath a banner declaring: 'For Freedom We Shed Our Blood' in Welsh, and joined the throng following David Jones uphill out of the town. As we left the houses behind to tramp along an unfenced open road, a red kite soared above us for several hundred yards in what many interpreted as an eerie gesture of solidarity.

The core walkers wore yellow T-shirts bearing the legend 'Listen to us' and were united in their opposition to a ban on hunting, but drawn from many different walks of life to participate in an extraordinary adventure that was enhanced by generous hospitality extended along the route of their march. Several of us from the Sinnington joined the converged flow of Caldbeck and Coldstream marchers for a day, north and south of Thirsk, and Mary Holt put her talents for entertaining to good use when the walkers rested for two days at her Ravenswick home. Apart from experiencing the Holts' legendary hospitality first-hand, James' and Mary's guests were also introduced to fireball hockey, which is the same as normal hockey except that it is played in the dark with a roll of flaming loo paper that has been liberally doused with petrol.

With the core marchers safely corralled in Hyde Park at the end of their long and arduous walks, the rally got under way soon after 11 a.m. on 10 July with a succession of motivational speakers who included David Jones, Lembit Opik MP and the actor, Jeremy Irons. Ann Mallalieu rose the hair on the back of a hundred thousand necks during a spellbinding address to the crowd that quite stole the show, and which will never be forgotten by any of us fortunate to have heard it. In her speech Ann spoke of freedom, a love of animals and the countryside, and the sacrifices made by those who had marched hundreds of miles to be there.

She ended by quoting Shakespeare's famous passage from *Henry V* to thunderous applause and set the seal on the most memorable of the many protests leading up to the ban, although they were all precursors of the mighty Liberty and Livelihood March through central London five years later that was supported by more than four hundred thousand people.

Back in Yorkshire we put away the kennels' bicycles and changed over to horses for the last three weeks of August, sometimes returning to the kennels after several hours in the saddle having been fortified by the hospitality of those we called in to visit along the way. Towards the end of that summer I was approached by two different hunts looking for an amateur; after eight fulfilling seasons in Yorkshire, the time seemed ripe for a move. Lord Daresbury and his joint master, Barry Woolham, came over from the Wynnstay's fabled grassland and hedges, where Robin Gundry was hanging up his boots, for a morning's hunting at Bowforth in early September, but their subsequent offer was conditional on my retaining the popular Bert Loud as kennel-huntsman. Having met Bert, I was not convinced that we would make the perfect team but, far more importantly, Richard Mould had given me his word that he would come with me wherever that turned out to be.

Four days after the Wynnstay masters had enjoyed a busy morning's hunting in Yorkshire, I drove down to Leicestershire to stay with Joss and Nicky Hanbury. By then I had already enjoyed several days' hunting with the Quorn, where my old acquaintance Fred Barker had for a time re-joined the mastership and was kind enough to send me on with the hunt's legendary professional, Michael Farrin, whenever I visited. I had experienced the delights of Muxloe Hill in the Monday country and enjoyed the wilder, hilly grasslands that reach from Tilton-on-the-Hill to the Elysian paradise that is Lowesby estate. I had judged their young entry a few years earlier and seen the sumptuous new kennels that had sent out a clear vote of confidence to the rest of the hunting world when they were completed in 1991. With the 'Father of Foxhunting', Hugo Meynell, as a former master in the late 1700s and a reputation for three consecutive centuries of superlative sport, there was really only one choice for me. On 2 October 1997 I was appointed by unanimous decision of the Quorn Hunt Committee to be their joint master and huntsman from 1 May the following year.

With arrangements for my future done and dusted, I was able to concentrate on making my last one in Yorkshire as memorable as possible. Following the sad loss of Hugh Murray Wells, I had also completed the purchase of Muscoates Grange, which lies in the heart of the Sinnington vale and lends its name to one of the best hunting coverts of them all. I moved into Muscoates in time for my last Opening Meet, complete with a chipped Belfast sink salvaged from Frank

Sturdy's farmyard that stands to this day as tribute to a devoted puppy walker and fine hunting farmer. It seemed like only yesterday that I had trotted past the very same house on my first morning's hunting with the Sinnington and watched Mrs Stamp herd her geese to safety before throwing hounds into Pilmoors covert.

We revived a tradition referred to in Herbert Read's book by meeting at Muscoates Grange for my final day in the Sinnington vale on 25 February 1998. Hounds had already run one fox to ground after a spin across Welburn and made a four-and-a-half mile point on another from Brawby to Riseborough at the opposite end of the vale when an outlier was disturbed from the Coulson drain at 4 p.m.. The pack ran fast over Normanby Hill before swinging south to Salton and doubling back behind Marton village, where Debbie Mould saw the fox cross the footbridge over the River Severn on to Podge Marton's Farm. The pack flew over the arable to enter Riseborough Hagg for the third time in just over a week and ignored a brace of fresh foxes as the hunt swung eastwards across wet, low-lying arable towards Pickering, to breach the Derwent boundary at Middleton and cross the A170 before continuing as far north as Cottage Leas. I wish I could recount that hounds had their reward after this fabulous 13-mile run that included a six-and-a-half mile point, but a combination of darkness and the intervention of a fresh fox at 6.20 p.m. put paid to any chances of that. Mary Holt was one of the few survivors and later gave me a framed map detailing every yard of the three good runs we had that day, the last of which was amongst the top ten low country hunts of the previous eight seasons. That evening I wrote in my diary: 'I am going to miss this lovely vale, so good to get about in with so few impediments to a long hunt'.

The remaining three weeks were spent, as is the custom, hunting the hill country, where we enjoyed a successful final outing to the Deer Park, which was by then under the control of game keeper Shaun Mintoft of the Ashdale drain escapade, and now a firm friend of the hunt. Visitors on the last official day included Peter Daresbury and his recently appointed joint master in waiting, Willie Wakeham, David Wallace and Amanda Hartington. Hounds pulled off a fine high-country hunt all about Nawton Tower and Riccal Dale, which ended when they caught the fox below Cowhouse Bank after an hour and three-quarters on a scent that was never better than holding. Five days later I hunted the pack I had bred for the last eight years for the final time after the hunt gallop at Douthwaite Dale. A field of more than a hundred horses was much diminished by the time we found our fifth and final fox of the day in Schoolhouse planation besides Stoneley Woods. The ensuing 7-mile circular hunt took in the cream of our wildest high-country sprawling either side of Skiplam's top end before scent became so faint that only Greenfinch '94, descended from the Old Dominion line I had been given by Ronnie Wallace, could own the line. It felt strange indeed blowing hounds up on the cusp of Boonhill Bank overlooking the brooding, dark mass of Bransdale Moor, knowing that it really was for the last time. With all hounds on, I slipped from my horse and thanked them for hunting I knew could never be bettered.

By the end of April a tenant had been found for Muscoates Grange and I was ready for the move to Leicestershire. James Holt generously and typically hosted a small farewell dinner at the Star Inn, Harome, and at the April puppy show I was presented in the pouring rain with a magnificent painting by Alison Guest. It depicts hounds running hard up the heathery slopes of Threadgold Bank with the whipper-in's hat held aloft and the wild, brown moors beyond: a timeless landscape of strong foxes and memories of great hunts as indelible as the hills themselves.

CHAPTER 12

Quorn – joint masters, hunt staff and hounds

In case I was in any doubt about the magnitude of my new undertaking, James Bouskell, who claimed a former Quorn secretary in Tempest Wade as a relative, kindly sent me a signed copy of Colin Ellis's 1951 book, *Leicestershire and the Quorn Hunt*, which offers an accurate and fascinating account of the hunt's illustrious history. Of the many anecdotes in the book, my favourite describes former huntsman Walter Wilson riding his horse down the steep railway embankment below Thorpe Trussels covert and quietly retrieving hounds from a terrible fate. The story gained poignancy when I discovered a plaque hidden amongst bramble and briars of Thorpe Trussels, which stands close to the Kirby Bellars kennels, commemorating Mr Bouskell Wade's gift of the covert to the hunt in 1977. There were many other letters wishing me well in my new venture; I was too busy to reply to most, but have never forgotten the kindness of their senders, who included Ronnie Wallace and the former Quorn Secretary, Jonathan Inglesant, who pledged his support and assistance. David Samworth wrote to say that we would always be welcome on his 400 acres of grass in the Friday country and Ginny Johnson from Quenby Lodge offered open house whenever I needed a bolt-hole, promising 'a fridge full of goodies', which was music to the ears of a hungry bachelor.

I had spent only three of the previous eleven seasons with a joint master; Tim Millar had stayed on to bed me into the role on Dartmoor, and Andrew Osborne's involvement was to put icing on the cake of an already well-oiled enterprise for my final two seasons in Yorkshire. I now had four joint masters to work with, each one responsible for field mastering on one of the four days a week that the Quorn still hunted. I already knew Joss Hanbury both personally and by reputation, for he was, and still is, a supremely elegant and brave horseman capable of nurturing the greenest horse across the most formidable country, although we had given him a ducking near Rookbarugh when he came up for a day with the Sinnington. Laconic, laid-back and shy, Joss had been shoved unceremoniously into the spotlight after the infamous Quorn video, which showed a bolted fox running back into the hounds to be killed, and paid a bitter price by being forced to resign the mastership. Many lesser men would have thrown in their hunting towel there and then, but Joss kept his head down, continued to lead the field across his beloved Friday turf and had resumed his mastership the season before my arrival. Above all, Joss was a genuine countryman, never happier than when buying and selling poultry at Melton market.

Several well-intentioned people had warned me that I would find Joss frustrating and difficult to pin down, but my experience was the exact opposite, for he was both supportive and helpful in every possible way. No one had any suggestions as to where I might live, but Joss found near-perfect accommodation at Windyridge Farm, which was within walking distance of the kennels. I found a note of welcome together with a basket of fresh eggs and vegetables the day I arrived there from James and Amanda Sparrow, who lived close by at Eye Kettleby Hall. My other neighbour lived half a dozen grass fields and hedges to the east at Cream Gorse, one of the finest coverts in the Friday country. Joan Crosfield became a firm friend and to walk across pastures run to seed in high summer and spend an evening with Joan and her wire-haired dachshund was a frequent treat during that first hectic summer in Leicestershire.

Monday master Charles Geary was the polar opposite of the Squire of Oakham, not that Joss was ever known to use the pretentious title that was his birthright. Charles ran a successful bakery and had been parachuted in to the mastership in the wake of mass resignations following the 1992 video. Since then, he had immersed himself wholeheartedly into the Quorn Hunt, and by sheer determination and effort made the well-fenced Monday country his own, although I felt that he never properly grasped the venery of the chase. Charles cleared country with due diligence in his large Mercedes car with a boot stuffed with loaves of bread that he dispensed amongst the farmers, kissing their wives on both cheeks. He was so popular that when he retired after eight seasons in office the Monday farmers presented him with a plaque stipulating that he was to hunt over their land without charge for the rest of his life.

Rad and Shirley Thomas lived in Charnwood Forest at Whatoff Farm, from which base Rad hunted, farmed and immersed himself in the politics of the NFU. The door was always open at Whatoff, the house and farmyard as refreshingly scruffy as their bearded owner, with whom I quickly established a good rapport. We hunted the heavily wooded and well-foxed Charnwood Forest on a Tuesday, where rocky outcrops tower above crystal-clear streams that are pure enough to support a healthy population of indigenous crayfish. To sit back amongst those surroundings and let hounds sort it out for themselves after the intensity of a Quorn Monday was often refreshing, although we were never far from the M1 motorway and ever expanding house building. Glamorous Monday and Friday subscribers rarely went anywhere near a country half as trappy as the forest north of Leicester, and most knew it only as the place where the famous Tom Firr sustained such a bad fall in 1898 that he never hunted hounds again. The joint mastership was headed up by Richard Carden, a retired banker from Sussex who lent gravitas and authority to our monthly meetings, rode bravely and maintained a small flat at Quenby Hall from which base he hunted two or three days a week and undertook field-mastering responsibilities on the seriously cramped Saturdays.

For much of my time in Yorkshire, Richard Mould was the only full-time professional, but things were very different at Kirby Bellars, where there were seven houses available for hunt staff, including two grand, detached dwellings for the kennel huntsman and stud groom that were separated by half an acre of immaculate lawn. One of these had been let out to a family that had no connection with the hunt, but was requisitioned with some difficulty for Kit Dwerryhouse, who left his position at Bramham Park in Yorkshire to become our stud groom after the initial incumbent departed halfway through autumn hunting. Kit had two girl grooms to assist, including young Emma Watson, who came down from the Sinnington country to help out for a season. In Neil Brooksbank, I inherited another Yorkshireman as terrierman, with Peter Loddington as the fence man. Neil was often perplexed by much of what went on in Leicestershire but was a real grafter and superb at a job that involved the longest and least-sociable hours of them all. The team was completed by David Sherwood, another gritty northerner who I had met during a foot day hunting the cliffs north of Whitby with the Goathland. David possessed all the attributes of a good kennelman and does that job to this day with the Tynedale Hunt in Northumberland.

From the moment of my appointment, it was clear that one of my greatest challenges would be taking over from the Quorn's long-serving professional huntsman, Michael Farrin, who had remained resolutely at the top of his game for a remarkable thirty years and, as I had seen first-hand, was as consummate a horseman in his last season as in his first. As a child I remember the Goathland huntsman, Derek Gardiner, cracking jokes about replacing Michael Farrin at the Quorn whenever he pulled off a good hunt, and as a young man I had devoured Foxford's thrilling accounts in *Horse & Hound* of hunts across high Leicestershire behind the Quorn bitches and their fearless huntsman away from coverts such as Curates, Ella's and Walton Thorns. It cannot have been easy for Michael to hand over to an amateur after such an illustrious career; however, he was unfailingly courteous and helpful throughout the changeover.

Michael had exercised the dog and bitch hounds separately, but both Richard and I were keen to dispense with that approach and from 1 May onwards the Quorn hounds were walked out together in one lot. We took the pack up the back lane that first morning and let them romp about amongst the rich May grass beneath a fresh north-westerly. Amongst the sixty-odd couple were several old friends from Yorkshire, including Beetle '97, Emerald '94, Stella '93 and Curlew '95, and a whole raft of strangers that it was my business to get to know in the coming weeks. They included Drummer '96, a fine third-season dog, handsome brothers Brigand and Brimstone '97, who were to win a first prize at the Peterborough Royal Foxhound Show that summer, and Charming and Credit '94, half-sisters by an old English dog from the Brocklesby. I had already worked painstakingly through my collection of stud books to trace the dominant tail female line to Mr Coryton's Ruby, which by a neat twist of fate led all the way back to the wild hills of Dartmoor.

CHAPTER 13

First impressions
at the Quorn

It was brought home to me before I even took office on 1 May that I could not assume the unqualified support of landowners that had been my gift in Yorkshire. With the permission of my future joint masters, I arranged to spend a day in early April looking at the hunt coverts with Neil Brooksbank, who was keen to show off the work he had been doing that spring. He was particularly proud of Grimston Gorse, which lies in the Monday country and had been given to the hunt in 1950 by the Wright family but was surrounded by Lord King's Wartnaby estate. When we arrived to inspect the fruits of a week spent covert laying with chainsaws, we did not find a mass of dense, green thorns as expected, but instead a bare, brown prairie blemished by half a dozen heaps of ash that had until two weeks earlier been living hawthorn. I could scarcely believe that a celebrated covert owned and maintained by the most famous hunt in the world could be so comprehensively vandalised under the watch of a man who was currently Chairman of the neighbouring Belvoir Hunt.

The upshot of our discovery was that Lord King offered to buy Grimston Gorse, but was told by the Quorn Chairman, Squire de Lisle, that the gift of the covert had been made on the condition that it must be returned to the Madocks-Wright family should the hunt ever wish to dispose of it. A couple of weeks later the Chairman received an extraordinary reply – dictated by Lord King but signed in his unavoidable absence – in which he describes the covert as being in 'ghastly condition and stuffed full of earth with no access to push foxes out'. His Lordship went on to say that he wished the owners would 'behave in a proper and responsible manner, which is not my experience of the Quorn'. As an incomer, I had no grasp of the history between the former Chairman of British Airways and the Quorn Hunt, although more than one person came forward to offer their own theories as to his hostility.

It seemed pointless to be crying over spilt milk, so I put the matter of Grimston Gorse behind me and at the end of May met up with the Wartnaby farm manager, Geoff Johnson, for a tour of the estate, during which it became clear that the Yorkshireman, who had been part of John King's life since the early days, was the rock that stood between Wartnaby and the Quorn Hunt. Whenever we came to a locked gate that morning, Geoff jumped out of the Land Rover to open it himself, determined not to divulge a combination that would open every gate on the estate. At the end of the morning Geoff signed off by telling me that I must contact him in advance of visiting the hunt-owned wood, but he had to back down when I pointed out that a public footpath ran through the middle. I wrote to Geoff the next day, thanking him for his time and expressing hope that we could enjoy successful hunting across the estate.

I received a reply soon after, in which Geoff wrote as to how much he enjoyed our morning together but also reiterated the fact that Grimston Gorse was part of a very important shoot drive. After managing the Sinnington Hunt coverts for eight seasons, I had firm views on how shoots and hunt-owned coverts should work, which was based on the need to leave them as quiet and undisturbed as possible. No shoot had ever been permitted to take over the management, release birds or shoot any of our coverts on a regular basis, although all were welcome to have a go just once a year and within forty-eight hours of being drawn by hounds. Where there was no shoot close by, I used to round up a team of hunt staff and local farmers and enjoy a jolly couple of hours beating out the thorns before heading to the pub for lunch. What was happening at Grimston Gorse was entirely different and, to my mind, completely wrong.

A month later the Kings invited me to dine at Friars Wells, along with mutual friends in Fred and Penny Barker. The evening nearly got off on the wrong foot when John King remarked to his wife, Isabel, 'I hope you haven't given him the best wine, he hasn't earned it yet', but he soon thawed and later took me on a tour of the house, pointing out a fine painting of his well-known hunter, Mr Wonderful. I was regaled with hunting stories from the days when plain John King ran a ball-bearing factory in the Badsworth country, and it seemed that his fondest memories were reserved for youthful outings with that sporting northern hunt. He also described in some detail how he had hurried round to Downing Street with a handwritten letter of acceptance having been invited to become a peer of the realm. Lady King was charm personified, and by the end of the evening we appeared to have reached an understanding that I could liaise with her about hunt access at Wartnaby. However, as I feared would be the case, I never was allowed to bypass the fierce guard dog that was Geoff Johnson. My efforts to encourage a good relationship with Wartnaby included inviting the Kings to have a look around the kennels one evening. Hunt staff were ready and waiting in immaculate, white kennel coats and bowler hats at the agreed time, but his Lordship never turned up.

Soon after my arrival I was granted an audience with Squire de Lisle at Quenby Hall; I never established what entitled our Chairman to use this title, but it was universally accepted throughout the Quorn country. It was clear that Gerard was not a foxhunter, however, he was certainly an accomplished and respected diplomat who stood some way off the day-to-day running of the hunt and spent several months each winter abroad. We chatted awkwardly in his oak-panelled study, during which I was given a superfluous map of Quorn meets from the 1920s, and afterwards enjoyed lunch served by a maid with whom Gerard conversed in Spanish. Sandwiched between Baggrave and Lowesby estates, the de Lisle land around Quenby lay at the very heart of the Quorn Friday country, was well foxed, and included the superb covert of Dixons Gorse.

Lowesby was owned by David Wilson, a successful housebuilder who was also the hunt treasurer and good friend to the hunt despite no longer hunting himself; we amicably agreed a five-figure budget for improving the country. David was too busy to show me around his stunning pastoral estate, but sent a note saying that I was welcome to 'tramp wherever I wanted' about Lowesby, where the gamekeeper, Mick Ward, had killed only three troublemaking foxes in a decade. The shoot at Lowesby was tiny in those days; however, there was a larger one at Baggrave, which Pam Scott had recently purchased from Asil Nadir. I found Pam to be equally helpful, although I could see that she would be a bad person to cross after we had spent an afternoon looking around Baggrave together and I drove my Suzuki jeep over a shallow ditch on to her drive. 'If anyone who worked for me did that, I would sack them', she said. I became firm friends with her keeper, Bruce Seymour, who was more than accommodating to the hunt and sometimes invited me to fish his trout lake on summer evenings.

With three large estates all well disposed towards hunting and keen hunting farmers such as George Coombes, who walked puppies for every pack of hounds in Leicestershire, it seemed that the Friday country required the least attention that summer. Instead, I prioritised getting to know the Monday, Tuesday and Saturday countries, which were all much more complicated. Charles Geary gave up a day a week throughout summer to introduce me to the Monday farmers, including the powerful duo of Bob Chaplin and Richard Greaves, who I met within the first fortnight of my arrival. Richard looked me up and down suspiciously and pronounced: 'He's too tall for a huntsman', but relaxed a little after Bob invited us into his small kitchen for a bite of lunch and a glass of port. Bob, who had cold, grey eyes and a habit of holding his hand at shoulder height whilst flicking his fingers, was the man any Monday farmer could turn to for help and advice regarding hunting on their land. The walls of his house were crammed with photographs of the Quorn Hunt in general and the Prince of Wales in particular.

Charles sometimes arrived with a picnic lunch in the boot, and when not meeting farmers we often took the opportunity to walk country and visit famous Monday coverts such as Curates, Parsons Thorns and Ella's, which had a line of delectable grass and fly fences running away towards Willoughby Gorse. If you look carefully, you can find a tiny plaque hidden amongst one of those hedge bottoms with the epitaph: 'The Prince of Wales broke these sticks', but on walking that country for the first time I was horrified to discover the famous hedges being fenced with sheep netting, which seemed strange considering that the land had been bought with hunting in mind by the indomitable Urky Newton. This discovery was made just in time to arrange for wide hunt jumps to be incorporated into the new fencing, nevertheless a little bit of high Leicestershire hunting country was never the same thereafter.

As I started to piece together the Monday country north of Leicester, it became increasingly obvious that there were large tracts of ground between favoured areas either side of the busy A46 and A607 where the hunt simply did not venture. I remember asking Charles what happened when hounds ran in a certain direction and he responded by saying that they were stopped; I knew then that proper hunting, as I understood it, would be very hard to achieve in the Monday country. There were other little incidents that set the alarm bells ringing, such as being told that the hunt paid £400 a year for the use of a vital wheat headland, and the reaction of a farmer on whose land lampers were destroying foxes. 'It's about shooting foxes down at the covert', Charles began when we met, but before he could continue, the young farmer interjected: 'That's no problem, Charles, just carry on as before'.

The fragility of the Monday country was further emphasised when the hunt secretary, Tim Hall-Wilson, called to warn me in early May that 'rumours were spreading like wildfire' about Fred Barker contributing to the cost of an evening for me to formally meet the Monday farmers. Tim sounded most vexed at this development, which I took to be the first of many storms in a teacup, and went off to shoot rooks in Triangle Spinney with the terrierman. They did things differently in the Monday country, where some of the best grassland was owned as an investment and let out for summer grazing. When Charles took me to meet Malcolm Portsmouth, who owned the famous line of big hedges away from Walton Thorns, he generously cracked open a bottle of champagne, and he was not the only landowner to greet us that way. Although champagne was not their style, Nick and Helen Connors from Upper Broughton were equally welcoming and a breath of fresh air. There was no side to the hard-working dairy farmers whose grassland around Muxloe Hill was the hunt's finest playground; they gave only hospitality, support and help that extended to planting nearly an acre of kale for our benefit beside the draughty covert of Hepplewhites.

I spent time too with Richard Carden and Rad Thomas, and could see at once that Saturday farmers such as David Cotton and John Adkin cared passionately about the Quorn Hunt, and were proud of a heavy, good-scenting country that lay either side of the M1, A6 and A42 between Loughborough and Nottingham but was severely compromised by these busy highways and every kind of urban expansion. Unlike the floating voters who subscribed to the fashionable Monday and Fridays, I was to discover that the Tuesday and Saturday fields were composed almost entirely of local people whose enthusiasm for hunting was matched only by their many and varied fund-raising initiatives. By the end of the summer, it was clear that I had taken on not one hunt but four, each with their own customs, loyalties and traditions.

CHAPTER 14

First season in Leicestershire

By the end of August I had met nearly all of the farmers whose land the hunt crossed and walked endless miles in my determination not to be wrong-footed when hounds ran. Richard had shown the young entry quite superbly to more than 250 guests at the puppy show, which was judged by Lord Daresbury and Captain Simon Clarke. After five weeks of mounted hound exercise – including some long mornings taking hounds around the Monday country – the corn was cut and we were ready to go. We hacked on to Ashby Pastures at dawn on the second day of September for a quiet morning below the radar and chivvied several foxes about before moving to Carringtons, where hounds roared around to catch a well-hunted fox. A busy morning ended with a short hunt from Joan Crosfield's delectable Cream Gorse, during which Lattice '93 shone in her work. The only disappointment was that Waggie, my twenty-one-year-old mare from Dartmoor, pulled out of her stable lame but she recovered sufficiently to hunt her third different pack of hounds a week later in Charnwood Forest. The next day we went to Gartree Hill, which had recently been acquired by David Wilson, where we had an altogether different experience.

David's farming tenant at Gartree had been unwell for many months and I had already been a victim of his hysterical and alarming rants, but the previous evening he had turned up at Joss Hanbury's farm near Oakham and physically attacked the farm manager. Now he drove up at 6 a.m. in a terrible and terrifying rage, during which his fire was directed at Richard, Joss and me in turn through a face contorted with hate and bile; I can only imagine what the large crowd of followers coming to see the new huntsman in action must have thought at this unpleasant spectacle, which ended as abruptly as it started when David Wilson appeared in his Jaguar to pacify his tenant. No sooner had that problem been resolved than another one surfaced when the former terrierman, David Johnson, took serious umbrage at the appearance in the hunting field of a past master of whom he did not approve. David roared off in his Land Rover, and was not seen again that morning. It was something of a relief to finally throw hounds into Gartree Hill twenty minutes later than advertised and get going on a leash of foxes; hounds ran more or less continuously for the next four-and-a-half hours, including a big circuit up to Burrough Hill that took in some Cottesmore country. When the morning ended, my thoughts were only for the hounds and their performance.

From then on, we went out five mornings a week throughout the autumn hunting campaign and covered as much of the country as possible. After the wilds of Dartmoor and Yorkshire it felt strange to be holding hounds up in a tunnel beneath four lanes of the A42 as the field spread out around Tongue Gorse, as we did in September, or to draw blocks of maize standing no more than two fields from the East Midlands airport and a few hundred yards from the racetrack at Donnington. Later that season we had a hunt from Tongue Gorse that ended when hounds caught their fox in a log pile at Middle Merril Grange Farm no more than a field from the A42 dual carriageway; to this day I cannot resist a backward glance whenever I drive past the scene of that triumph. We drew Grimston Gorse in early October but were not welcome anywhere else on Wartnaby on account of the shoot; the hunt covert was blank, but the morning was salvaged by a good show of foxes at Saxelby. An invitation to dine at Friars Wells was waiting for me when I got home, and when I mentioned this to Fred Barker, he remarked: 'It's not often that one is warned off an estate and then asked to dine by the owner within the same twenty-four hours'.

By the beginning of October we were letting hounds go and we enjoyed a fabulous morning from Hickling, where we covered a lot more ground than expected. I was riding a rangy bay gelding called Adam who Michael Farrin had chosen for his Neil Cawthorne retirement painting and jumped into a field of grass seeds belonging to John Copley, who was rightly very cross, and who insisted that I went back to tread in the divots myself. I did so the same afternoon and never jumped into a field of grass seeds again. We had also run all over Bob Chaplin's farm without prior warning, but he invited me in for a glass of port when I called to apologise and all was well. I summarised the autumn hunting by writing in my diary: 'What I have found most difficult is the inability to properly get about the less fashionable country on a horse, the bitches' reluctance to draw with enthusiasm and the doghounds' difficulty in settling to a line'. By Christmas I was to add that all a fox needed to do in order to save his brush was to run into one of the many villages or towns within our hunt country.

The Quorn have held their Opening Meet at Kirby Gate on the Leicester road out of Melton Mowbray ever since the days of Hugo Meynell in the late eighteenth century, although the venue was temporarily and briefly abandoned during the Masterships of Sir Harry Goodricke and Lord Stamford. The attractive façade of the house with its five distinctive dormer windows was depicted as a meet of the Quorn hounds by Henry Alken in 1824, when the now busy main road from Melton that is festooned with litter was nothing more than a track surrounded by rolling pastures in every direction. The present day reality is somewhat different, but the profound sense of tradition as we rode the short distance from the kennels to Kirby Gate for the Opening Meet on the last Saturday of October was heightened by 1998 being the Quorn Hunt's tercentenary year.

It has been the custom for as long as anyone can remember to hack four miles along narrow country roads to the first draw at Gartree Hill, although no one could explain why. The route meant passing the village of Great Dalby, which according to Joss Hanbury is the best hunting village in England. The outskirts of the village at Crownhill were also home to a small pit covered with thorns that Neil had laid the previous spring and which was separated from the traditional first draw by a dozen grass fields and hedges. The crowds of foot followers on the ridge between the two coverts got something of a shock when hounds appeared in full cry from behind them, but that did not prevent the fox being headed from his point of Gartree Hill. A busy day ended with a fast evening hunt from Joss's kale at Twyford to Baggrave, and I blew for home reasonably pleased with how the day had unfolded. However, that changed when I met Charles Geary back at the kennels, who was furious that we had ridden on to the meet without him at the start of the day. Until then, I had no notion that any protocol existed for all five joint masters to arrive at the Opening Meet together with hounds, nor would such a peculiar idea ever have crossed my mind.

As I had expected, the lack of traffic, conurbations or any other hindrance to hunting combined with free-draining, well-fenced grasslands, accommodating farmers and landowners and a plentiful supply of foxes made the Fridays a complete delight. Above all else the rolling green countryside east of Leicester and south of the Melton road was a land of space. I remember a wonderful day from Beeby in early November when the bitches caught two brace on top, the fourth fox being overhauled in the Lowesby gardens after I spotted Sinnington Heather '96 at a check, twice trying to worm her way through wire netting running through the middle of a very thick hedge. It was the turn of another Sinnington bitch, this time the second-season Beetle '97, to distinguish herself from the Markham House meet in January by bowling the fox over a hundred yards in front of the others after another good hunt across Lowesby. This took place in front of visitors from Yorkshire who included my old friends Michael Brown and Pete Teasdale and the event was recorded for posterity by Robin Smith-Ryland's pocket camera. After the day ended, Brian and Sue Henton kindly laid on a sumptuous hunt tea for all comers at Ingarsby, although the presence of staff was something of a novelty for my visitors from Yorkshire. Once everyone was seated at an enormous dining room table, Sue brought round a basket of blue duck eggs, which were well received by everyone except for Michael Brown, who told his hostess: 'I don't want any, thank you'. When pressed to change his mind, Michael lifted his doleful, brown eyes from the table and explained why he never ate duck eggs. 'The shells are porous', he said, 'They suck up shit from the ground'.

It was no surprise that the Prince of Wales chose the unspoilt Friday country for his visit on New Year's Day 1999, which was followed by a busy and eventful day, during which he rode up with me throughout. Things got off to a bad start when my horse ducked out of a big hedge and deposited me on the ground whilst the Prince flew over a set of rails to the side; I had no further falls but our Royal guest went on to buy two pieces of Leicestershire turf, although we both got safely over an enormous hedge with electric wire in front and a big drop behind on Harvey Whait's farm near Ashby Folville. Much later on, a fox slipped away from Andrew Coombe's kale then ran along the top of a heap of round straw bales, which Sinnington Stella '93 clambered up on to proclaim the line before Charming '94 took it away and the pack settled to run hard into the dusk. After a nice evening hunt ended at Little Dalby, I apologised for a run that had taken in more arable than usual, but the Prince responded by saying how much he had enjoyed seeing the hounds hunt. Our guest had ridden straight as a die ever since leaving the meet, appeared completely unfazed by a constant barrage of cameras and on the few occasions when they caught up with us, had a smile and kind word for the 'footies'. As we hacked home towards Little Dalby, the Prince pointed out the moon rising behind us over Gartree Hill, and offered some profound and poignant words of gratitude that I will never forget. Although I was to meet the Prince of Wales several times over the next eighteen months, that was the only occasion I had the privilege of his company as a huntsman.

If the Royal visit was a highlight of my first season, the next Hickling Monday in January was equally memorable, but for very different reasons. Considering the damage wrought by the Quorn video in 1992, it was hardly surprising that there was distaste and concern over terrier work; however, it has always been my conviction that foxes must sometimes be dispatched when run to ground. Fred Barker had banned the use of terriers altogether in the sensitive seasons following the incident, and I had unwittingly stirred up a hornets' nest of discontent by rewarding hounds with a fox they had run to ground in a rabbit hole on Hickling Standard at the end of a long September morning. That unlucky fox from Parsons Thorns was one of four-and-a-half brace we hunted that day. A few fields away on the west side of the busy A606 lies another hunt covert called Curates; as the old Meltonians were fond of saying in reference to finding foxes: 'If the Parson cannot perform the service, the Curate will'.

The land to the north of Curates was owned by Johnny Parsons, who exemplified the old-fashioned livestock farmer sometimes referred to as a 'stick and dog man' and farmed a landscape that cannot have changed much in centuries. As this covert was drawn pretty much every three weeks throughout the season I often marvelled at the farmer's benign tolerance as some two hundred horses paddled about on his sodden turf waiting for a fox to leave. The first time we drew Curates in early November a fox went away across John Copley's grasses and ran straight to the thundering traffic of the A46 Fosse Way, where I had no option but to stop hounds just as they were settling to hunt. We were back in the same area at the end of the month for a day when I drew the disused railway line from the opposite end to normal and was rewarded with a fox well found and a storming ride across Bob Chaplin's venerated hedges behind hounds in full cry. That gave me special pleasure for the normal practice had been to trot alongside the railway line whilst Charles led the field on a pointless jolly across country to meet up with hounds and huntsman at the other end.

We did not find the Fosse Way fox that day, but he was waiting for us the next time we drew Curates and the pack again had to be stopped before reaching the busy main road. At the end of January fox and hounds just beat us to the dual carriageway, but in an exceptional piece of whipping-in Richard leapt off his horse, ran up on to the busy road, halted the traffic and got every hound across safely. Unbelievably, a bridlepath meets the A46 within yards of where the fox had crossed, the place marked by a wooden hunting gate that we all filed through to continue the hunt. The fox had clearly got used to relaxing once he had crossed the road, for the next instant hounds were coursing him back over four lanes of tarmac. I like to think vehicles held up by the Quorn Hunt that afternoon gained some compensation watching us jump the central reservation before disappearing back through the same rickety hunt gate. Most unusually and much to my surprise, there was no fallout from the Committee, subscribers or general public in the wake of this unusual incident, which must have briefly delayed several hundred cars. When the fox found refuge soon afterwards beneath Johnny Parsons' ancient, wooden hen hut, there was no question in my mind as to his fate. I had no desire to cross such a dangerous main road ever again, yet here was a fox that had done just that on three separate occasions. Neil dispatched him within minutes; hounds had their reward and that was the last time we ran close to the Fosse Way for the rest of my short time at the Quorn. I have recounted the details of that memorable hunt many times since, citing it as a perfect example of when terriers came into their own.

Hunting on Tuesdays and Saturdays was less fulfilling but equally hair-raising as we tried to reconcile pursuit of a wild quarry with a veritable minefield of busy main roads and the tragic loss of hounds struck down and killed by speeding motorists. Despite the many lows, there were moments of fulfilment in these constricted lands, such as the occasion when we met for the first time in many years at the beautiful National Trust property of Calke Abbey in Derbyshire. During a hunt on a fox from Pip Hewitt's farm, the pack ran down to Staunton Harold Reservoir, where my old friend Tynedale Mayfly '91 carried the line single-handedly along the paving slabs that lie between the tarmac road and the water's edge. My thoughts went briefly back to a great hunt of the past that Mayfly had also saved, but those days felt like another life.

In addition to Richard Mould, I had David Bland to help out on Fridays and Bill Morris on most other days. David worked for the legendary Barbara Rich, who entertained hunting luminaries to generous hunt teas, saw life in black and white and sold many of the best hunters in Leicestershire. David was usually mounted on a nice-looking youngster from Barbara's Thorpe Satchville yard, but Bill tended to ride his own. One February evening there were just four of us left at the end of a moderate day in Charnwood Forest, including a lady subscriber who unbeknown to me had lent Bill a horse. I had seen it stop at some very small rails at Copt Oak, and generally give the little man an awkward ride throughout, so rather too loudly volunteered my uncomplimentary views on his new mount. To my surprise Bill protested the opposite, telling me with a look of acute embarrassment that it had the makings of a really good horse. Not for the first time, Rad Thomas came to the rescue, kindly pointing out that the horse belonged to the lady standing right beside me.

We eventually got to draw the Wartnaby coverts following a meet at Friars Well in February, after which Lord King kindly sent me a large, colour photograph captioned in handwritten ink of hounds moving off down the drive. We had a most unusual hunt in the afternoon when a fox from Little Belvoir led us at racing pace over the Roman Road and on past the site of Welby Osiers to the test railway line at Asfordby Hill. Here, siblings Diamond and Dingle '95 led the pack straight down the line and into a long, black tunnel, where they were soon engulfed by the darkness. I abandoned my horse, and leaving Richard to wait at one end of the tunnel, jumped into Neil's jeep to locate the other end. Eight couple eventually drifted back the way they had come, but Neil and I caught up with the others when they emerged into daylight, having gone clean underneath the busy A6006. We made it as far as the River Wreake and only a few fields from the kennels at Kirby Bellars before scent failed after a four-mile point. We hardly left the ground during this hunt, but it was one of the top five Mondays I ever had.

We held the final Monday meet at Bob Chaplin's High Holborn Farm in conditions that were so wet it was hardly fit to hunt, but the charity day went ahead at the insistence of the Monday farmers and raised a significant sum for division amongst three local churches. The last three Fridays of the season each produced a four-mile point, and I was delighted to receive a handwritten note of congratulations after the second one from Michael Clayton, who has sometimes overlooked my generation of huntsmen in his many books on hunting. The season ended with a new meet at the Symingtons' Seldom Seen Farm and a two-hour hunt in the morning from the Tilton Hills. We did not change horses until 2.30 p.m. and having drawn across Ingarsby, found in Keyham Rough and ran to Scraptoft Gorse on the outskirts of Leicester at Bushby. Before we knew it hounds were amongst the back gardens of Dalby Drive so I asked the stud groom, Kit Dwerryhouse, to jump off his horse and push them back to me. He emerged a few minutes later, grinning from ear to ear and brandishing the brush of our hunted fox. This was a good result, but I returned the next day to call on the residents of Dalby Drive and apologise for any inconvenience. To my surprise, no one objected, although the guitar-strumming owner of number 47 told me that his first thought on seeing the Quorn hounds in his back garden was that someone had loosed off a herd of pigs.

CHAPTER 15

Leicestershire summer highs and lows

After my first four days a week season with attendant railway tunnels, hunt politics, dual carriageways, motorways and the outskirts of Leicester, I was ready for a breather by the middle of March, but had somewhat rashly agreed to run the London Marathon in aid of the Countryside Alliance and the Royal Agricultural Benevolent Institution (RABI) for a second time under the banner of the Farquhar Fliers. Our team of eight runners included the Devon and Somerset huntsman Donald Summersgill, who drove up from Exmoor, ran the race and returned to the West Country all in the same day, and Luke Tomlinson, who was to become one of the Westminster Eight five years later. The team also contained two ladies: one was the amateur jockey, Gee Armytage, while the other struck up such a friendship with my old pal, Frank Houghton-Brown, that they disappeared off to the Turks and Caicos Islands together within twenty-four hours of crossing the finishing line.

Quorn Masters have benefited over the years from generous opportunities to entertain farmers who support the hunt, however, the dilemma has always been deciding which farmers should be rewarded for their ongoing support, and which should be invited in the hope that they might become a little more relaxed over hunt access. The Chairman of the Household Division Saddle Club, Barney White Spunner, kindly wrote to invite thirty hunt guests to the Beating of the Retreat at Horse Guards Parade in early June; the evening was a great success, made even more so when General Evelyn Webb Carter brought the Prince of Wales in for a drink afterwards, which one farmer's wife described as the icing on the cake. The Prince's memory for a face as he singled out various farmers and their wives for a chat was remarkable. He had not forgotten his day with us either, and repeated how much he had enjoyed the fast evening hunt on New Year's Day. His personal assistant had written to me within a month of that visit to invite forty farmers for a summer lunch at Highgrove in August, and as the Prince said goodbye he enquired with perfect charm: 'I hope you don't mind that the Meynell are coming too?'.

So it happened that eighty guests drawn equally from the Meynell and Quorn Hunts arrived at Highgrove eight weeks later for a quintessentially English summer lunch of Cornish crab and beef from the Highgrove home farm. We laid on a bus for the Quorn farmers, which left the kennels at 7.30 a.m. and arrived in Gloucestershire in time for a tour of the Highgrove gardens, which, despite several exotic immigrants, were immersed in an overwhelming aura of natural Englishness. The Prince met every one of his guests before we sat down to lunch, after which he spoke of his love for hunting and the freedom it engendered in him. Herbert Egglestone, a keen hunting farmer who lived close to the kennels at Kirby Bellars, stood up and offered an eloquent vote of thanks for the Royal hospitality just as Tiggy Legge-Bourke arrived with the two young princes.

In addition to a full schedule of puppy and hound shows, there were always other functions to attend, some more salubrious than others. The rook-pie supper in the Carrington Arms at Ashby Folville was a personal favourite, where every guest left the pub at the end of the evening with a small polystyrene tub containing a piece of cold pie for their lunch the next day. The main ingredient was shot by the terrierman from rookeries in some of the hunt coverts during early May, when there is a narrow window of opportunity between young rooks leaving their nests and learning to fly that has provided generations of countrymen with a sustainable harvest. Provided that the young rooks are shot on only one occasion, there are always plenty hatching early or late enough to replenish the population. There were also Pony Club visits to the kennels, drinks parties for each day of the week we hunted, and our own puppy show to organise, co-judged my second summer by Diana Scott from the Devon and Somerset Staghounds, whose sport was under even greater threat than our own.

Although the Hunting Act would not be passed for another five years, the pressure on hunting was gathering momentum despite the unqualified success of the Countryside Marches and Hyde Park Rally the previous summer. I was collected by a driver one evening in July and driven to the Central TV studios in Nottingham for a live televised debate on hunting chaired by the presenter Nicky Campbell, where the other pro-hunting speakers included Simon Hart and Julian Barnfield. The opposition boasted former hunt servant Clifford Pellow, who I clearly heard whisper under his breath, 'big-headed bastard, just like his father' when Simon spoke up in defence of hunting. It cannot have been a coincidence that a small group of Quorn saboteurs were seated directly behind me in the front row; one of them asked whether I had received his postcard from Greece, which had been signed 'Dave'. As the card was written and signed in an identical manner to several others that had been sent threatening arson to those kind people who hosted meets for the Quorn, I took this to be rather a stupid intervention on his behalf, and the matter was reported to the police the next day. The spate of threatening letters reminded me of one sent to my Harome address in Yorkshire several years earlier, which I thankfully opened with a paperknife instead of my fingers. The envelope concealed a red-stained razor blade together with a note that read 'the blood is AIDS'.

A few weeks later hunt supporters from the Saturday country organised a demonstration outside Belton village hall, where the anti-hunting Labour MP for Leicestershire North West was holding a surgery for his constituents. David Taylor MP emerged to find a hostile but well-mannered crowd waiting for him in the heart of Quorn Saturday country, but was outmanoeuvred most of all by Richard Mould, who asked him what plans were in place for his family to be rehoused in the wake of a ban on hunting. Mr Taylor's response to this sincere question was to ignore it altogether and quickly change the subject, but for everyone close enough to witness the exchange the encounter was a minor triumph for our cause.

The Quorn were faced with another huge problem following an announcement that Alstom had accepted a £1.2 billion order from Virgin Rail Group to build fifty-three new high-speed trains, which it intended testing along the disused railway line that ran through the middle of Bob Chaplin's grass farm. Upgrading the Old Dalby test track to include electrification of the line was expected to cost £24 million and there seemed little hope that the interests of the Quorn Hunt could be taken into consideration against the backdrop of such a huge project. I wrote to the train-testing company anyway, raising concerns on behalf of the hunt and pointing out that we expected to be operating in the vicinity several times each season. I was granted a meeting soon afterwards at the pub in Upper

Broughton, during which those present could not have been more helpful, but the practical solution of fencing the line against foxes seemed much more likely than being granted an undertaking to refrain from testing on a number of agreed Mondays each winter.

It was always something of a relief to have days when politics, socialising and administration could be put aside in favour of spending time immersed in the summer landscape of the Quorn hunting country visiting farmers and attending to some of the twenty historic and beautiful woodlands still owned by the hunt. Coverts such as Adams Gorse, Botany Bay, Curates, Herricks Thorns and Shoby Scholes had been providing foxes for the Quorn hounds to hunt for a century or more, their names part of the annals of the chase that resonate to this day amongst foxhunters around the world. It was hugely fulfilling to add another name to the illustrious list by permission of Nick and Helen Connors, who allowed us to plant up an area of rough ground between twin streams that drain the sporting paradise of Muxloe Hill. The two-acre site was planted with hawthorn whips paid for by the Quorn Hunt Supporters Club and named Tatters after the Connors' favourite hunting pony, who is buried beneath the turf. Volunteers organised by Neil Brooksbank planted the whips in early spring and over a hundred supporters came along to the official opening of the new covert in August, which was followed by a barbecue at Dell Farm. The *Melton Times* was on hand to report the creation of a new wood that would provide habitat for a wide variety of wildlife; the same paper also revealed the conservation benefits of covert laying in a different issue, with a colour picture of laid hawthorn flourishing beneath a clear blue sky. The story of Tatters has a sad epitaph, for the small thorn covert so carefully designed and planted is now surrounded in its entirety by a release pen that offers sanctuary to pheasants, not foxes.

Just occasionally I found my own sanctuary amongst the green fields of Joss Hanbury's farm at Twyford, where I was welcome to stalk and shoot rabbits with my .22 rifle. The entrails made perfect bait for the crayfish that abounded in the Twyford Brook, and the traps I set for them were so productive that the first cage was often full of the greedy crustaceans before I had finished setting the last. The crayfish were so delicious that I served up a bowl of them to Alan Duncan MP and his assistant when they came to lunch at Windyridge one summer afternoon to discuss saboteurs. There were also a handful of kind souls who often fed me – generously and informally – whenever I was passing, particularly close neighbours Richard and Millie Egglestone, and Kim and Fi Smith-Bingham, who lived in the neighbouring Cottesmore country at Knossington. The Johnsons at Quenby Lodge did me an even greater service by providing a retirement home for Waggie after the brave little mare had carried me for eleven long seasons.

CHAPTER 16

Second season
up to Christmas

After such a busy summer it was a relief to start hunting again on the last morning of August in Charnwood Forest, where the doghounds caught a brace on top from Rad Thomas's meet at Whatoff Farm. I was back onboard Waggie a fortnight later for a 6.30 a.m. return to Scraptoft Gorse, but hounds, hunt staff and Joss Hanbury arrived at the appointed time to find not one other mounted follower in sight. Without anyone to help hold up Scraptoft, we went instead into some lovely rough valleys nearby that were rarely hunted. We quickly got amongst foxes and enjoyed a glorious ninety minutes galloping across miles of inviting stubble, much to the delight of our foot followers who felt as if they were being treated to a private hunt. When we returned to Scraptoft two hours later, the latecomers were prevailed upon to help hold up, and pay greater attention to punctuality going forward. Looking across to the ominous grey bulk of Leicester and its distant skyscrapers standing like upturned matchboxes as hounds rattled round the wood was a surreal experience, especially when the view in the opposite direction took in some of the finest hunting country in the world. Moving off sharply that morning seemed to have done the trick, for there was a prompt turnout for the meet at Botany Bay two days later.

There was a van of hunt saboteurs waiting for us outside the kennel gates early the following Saturday for the fourth consecutive week. On the first occasion we were out on hound exercise, the next time we were parading hounds at Stoneleigh but were followed all the way to Hinckley, and on the third Saturday we were not hunting because of Burghley Horse Trials. Richard Mould beat them for the fourth time in a month by leaving the kennels at 4.30 a.m. for the meet at Bradmoor, where hounds caught three brace on top during a busy morning without a saboteur in sight. Whilst these small triumphs were gratifying, it was clear that the saboteurs were intending to give us as hard a time as possible, and that action needed to be taken if our hunting was not to be disrupted.

In Yorkshire the local constabulary had encouraged us to recruit and deploy stewards to uphold the law; however, their Leicestershire counterparts were not quite so keen. This was made clear to me during a meeting with the Leicestershire Chief Constable, David Wyrko, in early October, which Rosemary Samworth helped to set up. The meeting got off to an inauspicious start when the Chief Constable asked me to wait outside whilst he disappeared into his office alone with Rosemary for some time. I never did discover the content of their conversation. That evening Paul Latham from the Countryside Alliance called to advise that a police officer had telephoned him to probe allegations made by saboteurs that I was in some way involved with an unfortunate incident that had taken place in the Sinnington country during my first season with the Quorn. No charges were ever brought against the Sinnington Hunt masters, none of whom I had been in touch with since arriving in Leicestershire, but having put down the telephone I wondered whether there was any connection between the fantasy allegations and my meeting earlier that day.

Autumn hunting in Leicestershire was broken for a fleeting trip north to the Middleton, where Frank Houghton-Brown organised the first and only hunting competition ever staged in the UK, and asked me to organise the judging of an American-styled contest where individual hounds were identified by numbers sprayed on to their flanks. I returned after a fascinating two days at Birdsall to hunt hounds at Grimston Gorse, which was once again devoid of foxes although the morning was saved by a small block of kale I had persuaded Etta Madocks-Wright to plant back in the spring. Much to Etta's delight, her well-grown crop beside the Saxelby brook held two brace, although it was blank later that year after she had allowed it to be shot. In a sad epitaph to the hunting completion, Drummer '96, one of two doghounds we had taken to Yorkshire, was knocked down and killed by a speeding car in the Saturday country less than a week after distinguishing himself by finding a fox on Mount Ferrant at Birdsall. The Quorn country was really much better foxed than the north; however, we did have a completely blank morning at the end of October when the famous Monday coverts of Craddocks Ashes and Walton Thorns both failed to hold. I have known other close shaves in the north, however, that miserable morning remains the only occasion I have ever drawn blank as a huntsman.

James Barclay, who was a joint master of the Cottesmore, invited Edmund Porter to bring his Eskdale and Ennerdale fellhounds down to Leicestershire for a November morning in Owston Wood, so we asked them to hunt Ashby Pastures the same afternoon, which is the biggest covert in the Friday country and a wood that always benefits from a good stirring up. Richard and Millie Eggleston hosted a generous meet for more than two hundred foot followers, after which hounds performed well in an alien land many miles from their Lake District home. Edmund, who was for a long time Chairman of the Central Committee of Fell Packs, included Woldsman in his pack, a stallion hound many of us had seen exhibited at a Peterborough parade of stallion hounds that summer. Soon after moving off, a rather dopey Quorn fox passed within feet of Woldsman, who lunged at this quarry with such venom that it would nearly have been cut clean in two had his jaws connected.

My day had not got off to the best of starts when Brian Fanshawe telephoned at 8 a.m. to ask whether I had seen the morning's papers, by which he meant the *Daily Mirror*. Apparently there was a photograph of me, captioned 'You're an animal', together with an allegation that I had buried a fox cub alive. The reality was that the bitches had coursed a fox to ground in the middle of a grass field a month earlier during a morning hunt from Adams Gorse. As we had already found six brace, I asked Neil to dispatch the fox, but he was prevented from doing so by four determined saboteurs. Instead, we blocked the holes in order to return to finish the job later, which the *Daily Mirror* erroneously reported as burying a live fox cub. No rule of the MFHA or law of the land had been broken, but the incident was enough to spawn a few unpleasant letters, including one from somebody who wrote that they had intended hosting a meet but no longer felt able to do so. As both the writer and address were completely unknown to me, I did not lose too much sleep over such a hollow threat. The saboteurs and their colleagues were back for a Saturday meet at Rempstone; however, John Mills had kindly and generously agreed to help recruit and organise stewards, which the Saturday farmer did to such good effect that the 'sabs' disappeared within an hour to go to persecute a softer target.

We had another large hit by saboteurs on the first Saturday of December, which happened to be on the eve of our annual hunt ball. At one stage of the afternoon a sinister, masked face addressed me by Christian name and asked whether I had taken out insurance for the evening. By now well used to empty threats, I thought no more about it and continued trying to show sport against a backdrop of persistent and determined harassment. The hunt ball at Ingarsby that evening was such a sparkling and lively event that I did not get home until early the following morning, when I was accompanied by a particularly glitzy lady who Ginny Johnson had taken great pleasure in pairing me off with. We were greeted by my ashen-faced landlord, David Woodward, who told me that the 'antis' had attacked my house. Every single downstairs window had been smashed to smithereens but, far worse, my small terrier bitch, Floss, was discovered cowering beneath shards of broken glass suckling her week-old litter of puppies. From a public relations perspective the incident was manna from heaven and accorded front-page status by the *Melton Times*. It accurately reported £2,000 worth of damage, the trauma suffered by a nursing terrier bitch and the cowardly antics of thugs who saw fit to attack a private house when they knew the occupier would not be at home. The scene cannot have been very welcoming for my glamorous new friend from London, but she rolled up her sleeves and set to work with dustpan and brush.

Both dog and bitch packs had found top form by the middle of November, the dear beleaguered doghounds overcoming the many challenges of Charnwood forest to produce a fine seventy-five minute run in the Ulverscroft area that was a reminder of how special hunting must once have been across this land of sprawling woods and small pastures contained by neat drystone walls and thick, scruffy hedges. Not to be outdone, the bitches ran hard from Ella's to Prestwold the following week, reducing a field of well over a hundred to just eleven survivors including Vere Phillipps, who later told me he had jumped three hedges he had not seen since 1982. Knowing Vere's propensity for finding suitable obstacles in any country to challenge his well-bred hunters, I was not sure whether to take his observation as a tribute to the bitches' abilities or as an endorsement of his desire to travel off piste. Four days later the bitch pack produced a 12-mile hunt across the cream of the Friday country to cross the A47 into Fernie territory, but within a week they were coughing at the end of a busy day from Queniborough when we found a remarkable seven-and-a-half brace. There was no option but to suspend hunting there and then, but thankfully there were plenty of hunts willing to bring their own hounds to Leicestershire in order to help us out.

The Middleton came down to hunt the Hickling country in front of a large field that included Lucinda Green, NH jockey Norman Williamson and Tristan Voorspuy from Africa, who was destined to exert a huge influence over my life in the years to come. Ian Farquhar brought the Beaufort doghounds to Charnwood Forest on the Tuesday, despite having four other Gloucestershire fixtures to honour that week, and showed us how to do it by catching a brace on top after good hunts on a day when everything went right. Ian was especially pleased with the performance of a first-season dog by David Davies Bouncer '94, which he pointed out leading the pack into Stoneywell. The Beaufort had gone to the Welsh stallion hound for an outcross following Ian's success with Vale of Clettwr Fairy '73 during his time at the Bicester and Warden Hill two decades earlier. Willie Wakeham's Wynnstay pack of old English hounds put up a fine performance in strong winds from Great Dalby, while the Cattistock professional and former Quorn whipper-in, Charlie Watts, was greeted by foot followers in the Monday country like a returning hero. By the time our hounds were ready to go again ten days later, every visiting pack had caught at least one fox.

The saboteurs had lain low after their attack on my house, and with hounds fully recovered from what turned out to be a mild dose of the cough, there began a run of fine and uninterrupted sport. This kicked off with a sensational day following Pam Scott's meet at Baggrave in early December on a fox found in the Prince of Wales's covert, which was established by General Burnaby in 1871. The future King Edward VII was invited to sow some gorse seedlings, however, they failed to germinate and the covert was replanted by the General's executors after his death a few years later. The neat square covert has held foxes ever since, and this particular customer ran east into the best of our country at the charmingly named Carr Brigg beside the Queniborough brook. Our fenceman, Peter Loddington, had taken down miles of barbed wire protecting the Lowesby fly fences after the cattle had been brought in for winter, and the ride across those Elysian Fields with hounds streaming away in front and the hedges rushing in to meet us was as good as it gets. The hunt swung south across the Chairman's Quenby estate before hounds climbed up to higher ground at Sludge Hall to race in and out of the wild, grassy dales that comprise the Tilton Hills. We nearly lost them altogether here, but tired horses were granted a brief reprieve when our fox was headed trying to cross the B6407 on to the Partridges' big grass field. He got over on the second attempt and the bitches sorted it out to hunt on into the Cottesmore country as far as Tilton station, where the fox found sanctuary after a run of 14 miles and a five-mile point.

Not for the first time that season, we changed horses much later than planned, having moved them from the pre-arranged rendezvous in order to avoid wasting valuable time. An afternoon fox was hunted from Twyford to John O' Gaunt, a covert that was well established years before the nearby (and long since disused) railway line was ever built, and which is referenced as far back as 1835. Although my records clearly show this delectable thorn covert as standing well within the Quorn boundary, it has for some time been treated as a covert neutral to both Quorn and Cottesmore hunts. This was certainly the view most forthrightly conveyed to me by Rodney Vickers, who farmed much of the surrounding grassland, when he called at Windyridge late one evening to challenge me face-to-face over the Cottesmore's right of access. As I was wearing my dressing gown and Rodney was a little bit fired up, I thought it best to agree. According to the current Cottesmore master, Andrew Osborne, the encounter has never been forgotten.

A week later the bitches went one better to pull off what was probably the best hunt of my short time at the Quorn, and one of my top-five hunts of a lifetime. Following a hospitable meet at Carlton Lodge I took them to draw the late Mrs Ulrica Murray-Smith's unkempt garden where a fox was quickly away through Folville Spinney to Barsby, where the pack checked amongst sheep. I had taken a fall at the very first hedge, but arrived in time to hold hounds down the Barsby back lane and recover the line. Hounds settled to cross the South Croxton road by the Baggrave turn-off and pick away steadily across Richard Brett's inviting grass farm, where the fox was reported to be a good fifteen minutes in front. The pace increased as they ran on to Lowesby at Carr Brigg for the second consecutive week, but concerns over shooting were dispelled when a messenger galloped up to convey the welcome news that we were free to continue the hunt. Having run the full length of Lowesby, the bitches went over the Hungarton road, skirted the Quenby covert of Dixons Gorse and headed up into the wild Tilton Hills above Cold Newton before swooping back down to Lowesby by South Lodge having made a 6 mile point.

A hard-riding field could hardly believe their luck when presented with a second helping of the delectable Lowesby and Quenby estates, and when hounds checked amongst sheep at Church Spinney behind Hungarton the well-known Irish horseman and foxhunter, Aidan O'Connell, rode up beside me and put his arm around my shoulder. 'That's the best hunt I've ever had', he said in his soft Irish lilt, before adding quickly, 'outside of Ireland'. The words were no sooner spoken than the bitches regained the line to hunt across to Foxholes and down the brook beyond to an open earth a field shy of Keyham Bridge to conclude a remarkable run of two hours and twenty minutes. The annals of the chase are littered with stories of great or unusual hunts following the death of keen hunting personalities, most notably the Sinnington running to Robin Hill's grave the day after his funeral in 1958, as recounted by the Countess of Feversham in her fascinating book, *Strange Stories of the Chase*. I had only once met the Quorn's revered former lady master, but the 14-mile hunt across the very best of the Quorn Friday country was on a fox found in her old garden, the first time it had been drawn since her death in January 1999.

CHAPTER 17

Millennium and beyond

The Belvoir, Cottesmore and Quorn shire packs combined for a joint millennium meet given by the Melton Mowbray town estate on Saturday, 1 January 2000. A huge crowd of both mounted and foot followers gathered beneath bright, winter sunshine at the playing fields to hear the town crier, resplendent in his ceremonial robes, ask for silence in order that 'Mr Adrian Dangar, Master of the Quorn Hunt' could address the crowd. I cannot remember what I said, only relief that my brief words were well received. Despite considerable publicity leading up to the event, there was not a saboteur or protestor in sight. As I trotted from the meet with eager hounds clustered at my heels, it was hard to believe that the future of hunting was under such serious threat, nor could I have imagined that I had only four months left at the Quorn. The other packs followed their huntsmen away into their own countries; we had a busy day, finishing in the dark at Cream Gorse with just four riders remaining from the hundreds that had ridden out of Melton Mowbray that morning.

It was the turn of the Monday country to shine two days later when the bitches managed a 4 mile point in front of a hard-riding field of over two hundred that included more than thirty visitors. They had crossed the Smite to account for a fox in the Belvoir country before we found our afternoon pilot in a tiny, rough orchard I had discovered at the back of Upper Broughton village before Christmas. Plenty of saddles were emptied, firstly across Muxloe Hill and then over Bob Chaplin's hedges during an exciting ride that ended in the dusk at Bridget's Gorse. It was the habit of Quorn Monday subscribers to ride up and thank the field master warmly after a good day's sport, but this gratitude was rarely extended to the huntsman and his hounds. This was because a hard-riding field looked to the field master for entertainment that was often forthcoming regardless of whether the hounds were hunting or not, although the Brocklesby master, Lord Yarborough, was kind enough to write a much appreciated letter of thanks after the good afternoon run to Bridget's Gorse.

During my second season my thoughts turned towards securing a sustainable future for the Quorn Hunt. My joint masters and the hunt committee made it clear before my arrival that hunting four days a week in a country that had shrunk dramatically due to urbanisation and development was becoming unviable, and having hunted the country for a season-and-a-half I was in complete agreement. The Fridays were sublime, the Mondays tight, but the Tuesdays and Saturdays, about which I have written little, were impossible to hunt without serious and unacceptable compromise. On joining the mastership I had been asked to come up with a solution in my own time to an issue that was to divide the Quorn, for the problem was not disagreement over the three-day week in principle, but deciding which days of the week to hunt going forward. I had been in office long enough to believe that Mondays and Fridays were the unshakeable pillars of the Quorn Hunt; these two days suited subscribers and did not clash with the good ones offered by our neighbours. Indeed, it was still possible to hunt four days a week on Leicestershire grass if combined with a Cottesmore Tuesday and a Belvoir Saturday. But equally important was the fierce loyalty extended by our generous hosts to the land in which they farmed. The Monday and Friday farmers were subtlely different in their attitudes to the hunt, but both were proud of countries that had been hunted on the same day of the week for as long as anyone could remember. Many had fathers and grandfathers who had felt the same way.

Although the Tuesday country had its moments, hounds were never far from a busy main road and whilst generally accepting of hunting, large landowners such as Leicestershire County Council, Charnwood Council, the Woodland Trust, the National Trust and the Leicestershire Trust for Nature and Conservation imposed their own, often difficult, restrictions on sport. As huge swathes of the Tuesday country were open to public access and criss-crossed with footpaths in every direction, Rad Thomas and I were in complete agreement that hunting Charnwood Forest on a Saturday was out of the question. That left a Saturday country squashed between the sprawling conurbations of Loughborough, Leicester and Nottingham, and cut up into tiny segments by lethal main highways such as the M1, A42, A50, A6 and A512. If you throw in the East Midlands Airport, a motor-racing circuit at Donnington, several working quarries and a mainline railway, it is not difficult to appreciate that a once-sporting swathe of hunting country had by the millennium year become completely unviable for genuine hunting with hounds. Furthermore, the network of busy roads left us at the mercy of saboteurs, who returned to the fray with a vengeance six weeks after the attack on my house on a day when they were magnificently contained by stewards under the leadership of Gary Cracknell.

Despite the difficulties, I had put my back into opening up any part of the Saturday country where I thought we could squeeze in a day's hunting. We had met and hunted for the first time in decades at both Melbourne and Calke Abbey, and had ventured into the hills overlooking Nottingham at Kingston, where Richard Mould had to dismount in order to prevent hounds being shot at. After considerable soul searching, I concluded that the only way forward was to abort Saturday hunting altogether, surrender those areas that were a disaster in waiting, and concentrate on extending a few peripheral zones into the existing Monday country. In this way the well-foxed and accessible Prestwold estate east of Loughborough could form part of the Walton Thorns draw and provide space for longer and better hunts. Prestwold was owned by the mustard-keen Edward and Juliet Packe-Drury-Lowe, who have since parted company, but who always provided a warm welcome to their large arable estate. Subscribers were going to have to accept that Mondays could no longer be spent entirely on grass, and learn to appreciate the venery side of the chase, just as the neighbouring Belvoir managed to do during Martin Thornton's era as huntsman.

For all of these reasons I was convinced that the only way forward for sustainable hunting in the Quorn country was to hunt on Monday, Wednesday and Fridays. Under this arrangement there was still enough country left to provide a high standard of sport with minimal disruptions to farmers used to seeing hounds on certain days of the week, while the pillars of the Quorn Hunt would remain unchanged. If hunting just three days a week, it was impractical from a hounds' and horses' perspective to hunt on consecutive days, which ruled out any third day of the week except for Wednesdays. Under these proposals the country would be hunted by a mixed pack, with the emphasis on more bitches than doghounds. I could not see any other way of approaching the three-day week whilst retaining good hunting and sensible management of kennels and stables; with so much at stake, I felt it was crucial to go down a road that would result in the best possible hunting. To my mind, that was far more important than clinging on to traditional days of the week in country that was no longer fit to hunt.

The saddest consequence of this conviction was the alienation of several Saturday farmers and followers who were in many ways the genuine backbone of the Quorn Hunt. The Mondays and Fridays may have enjoyed the prestige and glamour, but the most successful fund-raising events invariably came from the tight-knit Saturday community. Farmers such as David Cotton from Diseworth, John Adkin from Belton and the Bonsors from Normanton had lived and hunted all their lives in the Saturday country, and doubtless retained fond memories of great hunts of the past. They and many others from that area such as the minkhounds master, Mark Shaw, had been generous with their time and help, although John Adkin was so fond of foxes that I sometimes found myself comparing him to hunting characters from Yorkshire who could not bear to see one killed.

I had sympathy for anyone who protested that abandoning Saturday hunting was unfair on schoolchildren and those unable to get off work during the week, but had no time for the flawed case of maintaining a noble tradition of Saturday sport. Although traditions are an important part of hunting and hopefully always will be, they should not be allowed to stand in the way of progress that is fundamental to the sport's survival; after all, hunting has been evolving constantly since the days of Hugo Meynell. It's an unfortunate fact that whenever amalgamations, boundaries or changes are considered there will always be a contingent who put their own interests ahead of the hunt, and when stating the case for change I was often reminded of Captain Wallace's wise words after I had been invited to join an MFHA subcommittee: 'Try not to think of what is best for your own hunt', he had told me, 'it's much more important to grasp the bigger picture'. By mid-January it was clear that there would be significant resistance to abandoning Saturdays, although nearly everyone accepted the inevitability of the three-day week.

We finally found a fox in the hunt covert of Grimston Gorse before the end of the season, even if I had to wait until the last day of February to do so. Lord King had given us a second lawn meet at the beginning of the month, where he parked his chauffeur-driven Range Rover so close to me that we could converse through an open window without his having to get out of the car. When Robin Smith-Ryland went up to the vehicle on foot and courteously introduced himself, he was warned: 'Don't tell me something I want to forget'. Robin is very seldom lost for words, but he was briefly stumped that morning. The very next day Eton '99 was mown down by a speeding motorist in Charnwood Forest while an even greater disaster was narrowly averted at dusk. Richard Mould handed his horse over to Darren Smith when he went off to fetch the hunt lorry, but Darren jumped up into the saddle without a moment's thought. Cocoa was a brilliant but highly strung mare who did not take kindly to her new jockey and promptly bolted flat out down the busy B591 in fading light. We could only watch, heart in mouth, as the mare vanished from sight to come crashing down on the tarmac nearly a mile further on; Cocoa was fine, Darren broke his hip. It could so easily have been a hundred times worse.

Hounds were thankfully in top form for Johnny Beardsall's visit to Lowesby on behalf of *Horse & Hound* in February, and did not disappoint when Rupert Uloth joined us a week later to report a Hickling Monday for *Country Life*. March was ushered in with a four-mile point from Gartree Hill to Marefield in the Cottesmore country, during which we were unable to change horses until 3.30 p.m.. The following day we had a final showdown with a particularly determined and aggressive horde of around seventy hunt saboteurs who arrived carrying home-made weapons and spoiling for a fight. Our terrierman had the keys to his vehicle stolen and the tyres slashed, and the head steward, John Mills, was set upon by a particularly vicious group of six during a day of running confrontation and tension that also resulted in a saboteur sustaining a broken nose. The reluctance of the police to prevent savage disruption to a lawful activity that day was truly remarkable, and so bad that Alan Duncan MP's constituency agent, Alan Deane, assured me that the issue would be raised in the House of Commons. The deployment of stewards allowed us to continue hunting, and hounds caught a fox in Vere Phillipps's covert, Polly, which was named in memory of his wife. At 3.30 p.m. the saboteurs threw in the towel and went home, leaving us to hunt in peace for the remainder of the day, which ended after hounds put up and quickly caught a large dog fox in a field of well-grown oilseed rape as we hacked home to Prestwold.

The season was all but over by then, with fund raising meets on the last Monday and Tuesday and a final lovely day across Lowesby and Quenby following the meet at Seldom Seen Farm. True to form, the Friday country did not disappoint and was as well foxed at the end of the season as at the beginning. We found a respectable six brace on top, and caught a well-hunted one at 5 p.m. as he tried a stopped earth in the delectable Tilton Hills. A week later we journeyed north for an invitation day at Birdsall in the Middleton Hunt country, which was supported by subscribers including Brian and Sue Henton, Andrew and Jane Collie, Helen Connors, Noel Pegge, Etta Madocks-Wright and Mary Samworth. Hounds winded a fox on the way to the meet at Wharram farm on top of the wolds, when only Richard Mould's sharp whipping-in prevented a premature find. Thankfully he was still there half an hour later and provided a lovely ninety-minute hunt before being marked to ground at North Grimston. A busy day amongst genuine foxhunters and open vistas of rolling pasture and wolds ended on the Garrowby march above Aldro at 6.30 p.m. I can still hear Richard calling hounds as I blew them up in the gloaming, and see the pale shapes taking form as they emerged in dribs and drabs from a steep, dry valley to curl up on the short grass beside my horse's heels. I did not know it then, but that was destined to be the last time I hunted hounds for eleven long years.

CHAPTER 18

Resignation

With the season over, there was suddenly time for various issues that had been simmering away beneath the surface to be given a proper airing. Apart from travelling south to help us out during the cough, the Middleton hounds had returned for a third visit in January to fulfil a long-standing exchange of days that included our own trip north to Yorkshire. When the hunt treasurer and Chairman of the finance and general purpose committee got wind of the intended Ingarsby meet, he objected most strenuously to the fact that our visitors would not be expected to pay a cap, and threatened to deny access to Lowesby that day. Huge embarrassment was averted at the last minute thanks to the diplomatic interventions of Charles Geary and Richard Carden, after which David Wilson wrote 'in the interests of the Quorn Hunt', to withdraw the threat of a ban.

However, he informed Richard Carden in the same letter that the hunt secretary had been instructed to withhold £50 for every visitor from Yorkshire from the master's guarantee, which was spent chiefly on paying our five full-time members of staff. The reality was that the Middleton had already contributed to the Quorn Hunt coffers by travelling down from Yorkshire at their own expense, which allowed us to honour lucrative December fixtures. A raid on the master's guarantee did not materialise in the end, however, an unhappy consequence of the incident was the decline in my much-valued relationship with our conscientious treasurer and generous hunting host. David Wilson had always been keen that hunting and shooting should work together, and I had enjoyed some of the best hunting of my life across his Lowesby estate. Nor had I forgotten the firm and unequivocal manner in which he had handled his raging tenant at Gartree Hill, and on subsequent occasions. David was gracious enough to host a lawn meet at Lowesby a month after the Middleton visit at which we chatted amicably as if nothing had ever happened.

There was little doubt in my mind that our salaried hunt secretary, Tim Hall-Wilson, had the ear of both David Wilson and the hunt Chairman. I had never enjoyed an easy relationship with Tim, who I felt resented the presence of a full-time master to rock his own steady boat. My appointment together with an undertaking to employ the staff and manage the hunt coverts considerably lightened Tim's workload, but his generous salary remained the same. I was not the only one to believe that he was overpaid and poor value for money, especially when Anne Creed did all the hunt typing and paperwork in a purpose-built office at the kennels. Obtaining signatures from farmers and landowners to authorise the use of stewards took up a huge amount of my time, and I could have done with the hunt secretary's help in this arduous task, but none was forthcoming. Things had come to a bit of a head during September, when I was especially busy hunting at least five early mornings a week. After several polite requests had fallen on deaf ears, I sent the hunt secretary an exasperated fax demanding that an expensive leak at the kennels be resolved by nightfall; he retaliated angrily with some demands the mastership were not prepared to meet. Tim was soon to leave the employ of the Quorn Hunt, but our mutual distaste for one another could only have conspired against me when the going got tough in April.

A chain of events was set in motion by a meeting of the finance and general-purpose committee on 9 April that was held on a date when I was unable to attend. The meeting was ostensibly called to discuss events surrounding a saboteur hit in early March, but developed into a full-blown critique of several wide ranging issues relating to the past season, which was universally recognised as having been one of fine sport and long hunts. The old adage that all grumblers are silenced by a run of good sport did not seem to apply to the Quorn, where some committee members did not ride to hounds and were therefore estranged from the reality of what went on in the hunting field. After Richard Carden updated me on my return from holiday, it was hard not to interpret the meeting as an attack on some of my key policies, which I had been unable to explain or defend on account of my absence. I had a very brief meeting with Gerard de Lisle on 17 April, at which he did little more than hand me a letter.

I pulled up on the verge of the Quenby drive to digest its contents a few minutes later and was horrified to discover that the letter amounted to a written warning regarding my conduct. Amongst other things, the Chairman objected to not being kept abreast of any incidents that could impact on the Quorn Hunt, but he could not have realised that I had to deal with a wide range of issues on an almost daily basis. These included constant allegations regarding the illegal stopping of badger setts and terrier work, and complaints whenever hounds ran near to villages, which was a frequent occurrence. It was the lot of the modern master to deal with these difficulties to the best of his ability, and I did not consider it appropriate to disturb the Squire on a weekly basis throughout his lengthy sojourns abroad. The Chairman also wrote that the use of stewards must be authorised by the committee going forward, which I took to be a slap in the face of all those volunteers who had given freely of their time to help protect the hunt. Others spent countless hours helping to obtain signatures from farmers and landowners authorising the use of stewards. Against the backdrop of the Squire's disagreeable letter was a raft of other issues that had crystallised since the end of hunting, most significantly a refusal to sanction the joint masters' proposals for the three-day week. Instead, the issue was to be delayed by the implementation of a working party, which would mean another whole season disaster-dodging on vulnerable Tuesdays and Saturdays.

There had also been a proposal that the four days of each week should be represented on the committee by a farmer from each country, however, the list of names submitted in writing to the Chairman on 23 March included the man who had threatened to attack Richard Mould and me at Gartree Hill sixteen months earlier as the Friday farmer's representative. Time is said to heal all wounds, but I was unhappy to serve a hunt that included on its committee someone who had behaved in such an appalling manner. Richard Greaves' letter stated that the nominations had the support from farmers in each of the relevant countries, yet Nick Connors, who probably welcomed the Quorn Hunt across his land on Muxloe Hill more than any other, told me that he had never been consulted. The worm had turned, and there was something rotten going on within the hunt.

I attended a meeting at Quenby on 26 April along with the MFHA Chairman, Lord Daresbury, Gerard de Lisle and Richard Carden, at which I handed Gerard my detailed response to his own letter of warning, together with my resignation as the Quorn Hunt's joint master and huntsman. Gerard left the room to read it alone and returned some minutes later visibly shaken. During the lengthy meeting that followed, Peter Daresbury expressed hope that I would reconsider, and was robust and critical of the way recent events had been handled by the hunt Chairman. Despite the awkwardness of the situation the meeting was not without moments of humour; when I was trying to identify by name a pack of draghounds that had been invading our country, Gerard, seeking to help me out, suggested the Oakley Foot, to giggles of suppressed laughter.

I drove up to Yorkshire to stay with my parents the next day, quite sure of my decision to resign, which had been made after close consultation with Richard Mould, who assured me in his own pragmatic way that he was happy to take on hunting the Quorn hounds should he be asked to do so. There were other difficult conversations to have, particularly with Etta Madocks-Wright, who had recently been appointed to join our mastership on 1 May along with Richard Hunnisett. At that stage neither was sure that they would continue. At the committee meeting in Leicestershire that evening, Rad Thomas read out my letter, made an impassioned speech and then left early to a standing ovation. Copies were also circulated to members of the committee, who were asked to sign a confidentiality agreement not to disclose its contents before the copies were collected up again. The upshot of the meeting was that Richard Carden was asked to form a new mastership that might or might not include myself.

Events moved quickly the next day. The three joint masters fell into Richard Carden's line and agreed to stay; I was pleased that they had done so for the good of the hunt, and had made it clear to all of them that this was my battle, not theirs. Richard Carden telephoned with his version of the previous evening's events but I sensed that his enthusiasm for my staying on had waned a little; he now knew that Richard Mould would carry the horn if asked. He warned me that the hunt was divided into two distinct camps, and that if I reconsidered my resignation, my supporters would rejoice but my detractors would make life very unpleasant. Before our conversation ended, Richard made it clear that if I were to come back, my return would have to be unconditional. He pleaded patience, and believed that everything I was advocating would come to pass in the fullness of time. The telephone was red hot throughout the day as a succession of supporters called and prevailed on me to reconsider, although there was no word from either Joss Hanbury or Rad Thomas.

All the rowing and unpleasantness, much of it initiated by people who knew little of the hard work and passion beneath the surface of a successful hunt, suddenly seemed a very long way from my fundamental love of hunting, hounds and the countryside. Richard and I walked out the hounds together one more time, when my heart sang as I watched them race ahead, only to spin round and gallop back, sterns lashing with excitement, their mood brim full of energy and confidence following a month's rest. As always, abandoning them was my greatest blow. I had given the Quorn Hunt my all, but the level playing field I had worked so hard to achieve had become a flawed and impossible pitch. I let my resignation stand.

Top: An autumn hunting morning with the Quorn hounds near Quenby surrounded by a sea of old grassland, October 1999.

Bottom: Autumn hunting with the Quorn at Prestwold, September 1999 with Loughborough in the background. *(Ray Paulson)*

Clockwise from above: Edmund Porter and the Eskdale and Ennerdale hounds leaving Gifford Lodge on their way to draw Ashby Pastures, November 10th 1999.

Quorn meet at Baggrave Hall, December 10th 1999.

Quorn hounds on summer exercise. Neil Brooksbank (left), the author and Kim Smith-Bingham.

Richard Mould on Cocoa at the Quorn.

Top: Tristan and Cindy Voorspuy with hounds and hunt staff at a meet of Ginger Bell's hunt at Deloraine, their house on the edge of the Rift Valley in Kenya, October 2001.

Bottom: The end of a successful hunt with Mr Bolan's hounds in Trinidad, January 2001.

Clockwise from above: Hunting mountain lion near Battle Mountain, Nevada in 2008. Grosvenor Merle-Smith on left, Jace Albati on right.

The Grand Canyon Hunt in Arizona, March 2008.

First morning back after an eleven year break from hunting hounds, September 7th 2011. *(www.mark-egertonimages.com)*

John Cranage, Sinnington Hunt amateur whipper-in. *(www.mark-egertonimages.com)*

Clockwise from right: George Lupton
shooting at home in North Yorkshire,
aged 94.

Sinnington hounds in full cry,
2011 – 2012 season.
(www.mark-egertonimages.com)

Sinnington hounds on the line.
(www.mark-egertonimages.com)

Peter Easterby, James Holt
(hunt chairman) and Dick Scott
at a Sinnington hunt puppy show
in the nineties.

Above: The meet at Griff Farm, January 4th 201
(Lucy Saggers)

Left: The author's wife, Rachel, leading the fiel
on a Sinnington high side day in 2013.

Right: Rachel with the Spooners near
Fur Tor on Claire Bellamy's last day
hunting those hounds, April 9th 2016.

CHAPTER 19

Hound shows and puppy shows

For the first time in thirteen years, I woke up on 1 May 2000 without a pack of foxhounds to go and walk out. I kept on the small rented farmhouse at Windyridge for the summer, but moved into a plush London residence at Elvaston Place to be with a kind and beautiful baroness. Floss came too, and overnight I traded the pursuit of foxes across high Leicestershire for squirrels in Hyde Park, but despite going for a dawn run around the Serpentine every morning we never succeeded in catching one. Farmers' suppers, hunt balls and Leicestershire dinner parties were replaced by a whirlwind of the capital's most exclusive soirees, including Conrad Black's summer drinks and glamorous Cartier evenings at Annabel's. I buttonholed Michael Portillo for his views on hunting at the former and spilt a glass of red wine down David Frost's dinner jacket at the latter, but he forgave my clumsiness with gentlemanly charm.

I may have resigned the mastership, but there were still puppy show judging commitments to honour, and obligations to the Peterborough Royal Foxhound Show, where Dermot Kelly had asked me to take over stewarding the bitches a couple of years earlier. Sometimes referred to as the Temple of the Foxhound, Peterborough has a unique atmosphere that sets it apart from other regional hound shows, and is often the setting for a showdown between champions from Ardingly, Harrogate and Builth Wells. Unlike puppy shows where bowler hats are traditionally worn only by judges and hunt staff, gentleman members and their guests are encouraged to wear this formal headgear, along with grey suits and stiff, white collars, although only a few regulars, judges and stewards continue to endure the latter. Masters of every pack in the country are encouraged to support the show by becoming Vice Presidents, which allows them to reserve the same ringside seats year after year and take lunch in the Vice Presidents' tent, although many prefer the informality of a sunny picnic in the car park; for some years now the Warwickshire and VWH hunt gatherings have been regarded as amongst the best.

The first Peterborough Hound Show was held under the guidance of the same Thomas Parrington who lies buried at the Sinnington Hunt's spiritual home of Kirkdale church and who was their MFH from 1879 to 1884. When secretary of the Cleveland Agricultural Society, Mr Parrington initiated the first open hound show ever held at Redcar in North Yorkshire, which was contested by the Fitzwilliam Hunt from Milton (as distinct from the Fitzwilliam family's other private pack at Wentworth Woodhouse in South Yorkshire), but which looked likely to fold following Mr Parrington's retirement as secretary of the Yorkshire Agricultural Society. This calamity was averted by a move to a new site at Peterborough in 1878, which was owned by the Fitzwilliam family, who have remained intimately associated with the show ever since. Thomas Parrington was one of three judges who officiated at the first Peterborough Show, the others being Lords Coventry and Macclesfield.

For many years the foxhound show was run in tandem with the East of England Show, but the two became separated in 1999 when the agricultural event was brought forward in deference to increasingly early harvests that kept farmers and their families away in July. For a few months either option appeared unthinkable to many of us who had shown and judged at Peterborough; we were concerned that the show might be a shadow of its former self without the hustle, bustle and crowds of the agricultural show, but would lose all prestige and championship status if relegated to an earlier date. The wise decision to retain the third Wednesday in July and later consolidate the show into a celebratory festival of hunting has stood the test of time to such good effect that Peterborough – as it is universally referred to by hunting enthusiasts around the world – is more popular than ever.

I had first shown hounds at Peterborough during my time at the Sinnington, and remember driving back to Yorkshire past combines busy in the cornfields with the Middleton MFH, following a memorable day when our entries had both won first prizes. I was invited to judge the doghounds for the first time with Robin Gundry in 1994, when we awarded the Championship to the eye-catching Exmoor Greatwood '93. As well as identifying unentered hounds as they come into the ring and announcing the results, the ring steward must also make sure that at least one eligible entry for the special prizes in each class remains in the shake-up. He must insist that only a single entry is put forward by each pack for the unentered championship, and ensure the correct cups and trophies are dispensed to the right masters and puppy walkers when they are invited to collect their prizes. If he is lucky, the humble ring steward may be invited for a drink at Milton afterwards, where the hound show committee gather discreetly behind closed doors to decide the following year's judges before joining other guests in the great hall.

It was particularly satisfying to win a morning class with a couple of Quorn doghounds before my afternoon debut as the bitch steward to Martin Scott and Lord Daresbury in 1999, my task that day made so much easier by the charming show secretary, Roy Bird, and by the great efficiency of assistant ring stewards, Tony Collins and Brian Gupwell. In 2004 I combined the roles of senior doghound judge, where Tim Easby and I awarded the championship to the Duke of Beaufort's Bailey '03, with a busy afternoon stewarding. My twelve years as a Peterborough ring steward came to an end in 2012, when I was unable to perform stewarding duties having accepted the committee's invitation to judge the bitches with Charles Shirley-Beavan; Tom Naylor Leyland took over that summer afternoon and has been doing an excellent job ever since.

The other regional shows may not have quite the same gravitas as that of Peterborough, but all are charming in their own particular way. The summer showing season is heralded by the South of England Hound Show at Ardingly in early June, which I first judged with Adam Waugh in 1998. I stayed with Richard and Penny Carden on that occasion, but Rachel and I were billeted with Peter and Anne Cairns for a return fifteen years later, where we enjoyed watching a litter of well-grown cubs gambolling beneath late evening sun in front of the Cairns' secluded and beautiful cottage on the eve of the show. The Wales and Border Counties Hounds Show at Builth Wells comes next, a stand-alone spectacle of hounds and hunting held at the Royal Welsh showground three weeks after Ardingly, where pure Welsh hounds are shown in their own ring with woolly sterns and chins supported by the exhibitor. The show is run by Johnnie Andrews with assistance from his son, James, who is showing good sport as master and huntsman of the South & West Wilts, whilst somehow managing to work as a land agent in Carmarthenshire. As the classes are held outside, Builth Wells has always been at the mercy of the weather but that has never dampened the enthusiasm of supporters, who gather after judging has finished to raise the proverbial roof with hunting songs from the Welsh hills and Lakeland fells.

The Great Yorkshire Show at Harrogate is held under cover on the Wednesday of the huge July agricultural show, and being centrally located benefits from a steady stream of visitors throughout the day. Whatever our prospects, the Sinnington never failed to support the show under my mastership, and we often returned with some red rosettes. The Sinnington's greatest day at Harrogate was during my final summer as master when Captain Ronnie Wallace selected Elder as doghound champion, which Jim Meads pointed out in his report for *Horse & Hound* was the first major championship the Sinnington had ever won. The seal was put on a memorable day when we finally overcame our illustrious neighbours, the four-day-a-week Middleton Hunt, to win the coveted Mary Furness memorial trophy for the most successful Yorkshire pack at the 1997 show. The Sinnington would have run out clear winners of the same award many years later when winning three of the four classes for unentered hounds in 2012, but were pipped at the post by the Grove and Rufford, who claim Yorkshire heritage by virtue of hunting a tiny corner of that huge county. When I suggested at our committee meeting that eligibility for this award should be defined by where a pack of hounds is kennelled, Jamie Cameron spoke passionately in favour of the hunt where his wife was once master and the rules stayed put.

As it is held in August, a few weeks after the show at Peterborough, there is a relaxed, West Country ambience to Honiton that makes it an especially charming show to visit. Hounds are shown in the open air, nobody except for the judges and stewards wears a suit, and many of the competing packs are shortly about to commence hunting. I was invited to judge there with Alastair Jackson at the end of my first summer in Yorkshire, where we made the controversial decision to award the bitch championship to VWH Hannah '88 ahead of Captain Wallace's Peterborough Champion, Exmoor Ripple '89. The *Horse & Hound* correspondent questioned the wisdom of showing a hound who has 'won the highest honours' but tactfully pointed out that 'many remote from Peterborough may like to see what a champion looks like'. No one does entertainment quite as well as the West Country, so there was much ribbing and further fun and games that evening at a party hosted by Rosie Taylor in her beautiful house at Cricket St Thomas, which was also the setting for the TV show, *To the Manor Born*. Despite our concerns, Ronnie Wallace accepted our decision gracefully, and six years later was kind enough to invite me to judge his own lovely young entry on Exmoor.

For a number of years I flew over to Düsseldorf for a weekend during the busy summer showing season to help judge the German hound show at Schwarzenstein, which was organised by Günter Dorken at the Rheinisch-Westfälischer Schleppjagdverein Hunt kennels. During the show, which usually lasts all day beneath a blazing-hot sun, foxhounds and beagles are considered by English judges in separate rings, with the young entry graded according to their looks. Members and friends of the German Drag Hound Association looked after us generously inside the small, ivy-clad castle that also serves as the hunt's clubhouse, but huntsmen lacked the empathy and skill of their British counterparts when it came to presenting hounds in the show ring. Occasionally one could be persuaded to let his charges off their leads so they could respond to a biscuit thrown across the flags, but most huntsmen preferred to keep hold of their hounds. I often thought that it would be beneficial for a delegation to attend Peterborough and see how hounds are shown in England; some German hunts had recently imported English hounds, which certainly stamped class on their progeny. It was traditional for the host hunt to run a short drag after showing was finished for the day, and I asked one year to join them. Hounds scorched away through the woodland on a breast-high scent, whilst the field rode behind in a hierarchal order that was the polar opposite of the cut and thrust of the hunting field back home. Not for the first time, I made a connection between hunting an artificial scent and the club mentality that so often accompanies it.

The prevailing high standards encountered in the British show ring have done much to promote and develop the foxhound as a breed, for a hound with good conformation is more likely to enjoy a longer working life than one that is over at the knee or weak behind. I have never understood the refrain, 'we breed ours for work, not show', for any person vested with the privilege and honour of breeding a pack of hounds should do everything possible to produce hounds that look good *and* hunt well. However, a desire to succeed in the show ring should never be taken so seriously as to jeopardise friendships or induce foul play, but there are occasionally examples of these unhappy occurrences. Richard Sumner, a fine horseman, previous joint master of the Heythrop, and former breeder of their unquestionably lovely hounds, was most put out when we preferred VWH Summer '11 ahead of his own contestant in the shake-up for the bitch championship at Peterborough in 2012, and he mentioned this dissatisfaction when we next met. Charles Frampton became master and huntsman to the Heythrop the same year and later agreed to buy Richard's house. On being shown round, he noticed an image of the same two protagonists occupying pride of place in Richard's kitchen, one of them presented to appear conspicuously more attractive than the other. 'That's to remind me what a bad judge Adrian Dangar is', Richard explained, still sore over Raspberry's Peterborough defeat.

As they offer up a captive audience, hound shows have always been a good place at which to get a political or other important message across, and I remember when the Chief Executive in waiting of the Countryside Alliance came into the Harrogate ring after the doghound championship in 1999 to address the crowd. As Richard Burge was a zoologist and reputed to be a paid-up member of the Labour Party, his appointment to steer hunting through the most turbulent waters of its history caused consternation in some quarters. Others viewed his selection as a savvy move and a welcome departure from the 'old school tie' and military-background brigade, although it was not widely broadcast that Mr Burge was the son of a colonel in the British army. This was the first time we had seen him in the north, and Richard won over many hearts that morning with an impassioned and well-received speech; the loudest cheer of all – and a standing ovation – was reserved for his pledge not to condemn the terriermen. This was particularly welcome news at Harrogate, for the hound ring on the third day of the Great Yorkshire Show has always been devoted to a working terrier show.

Things are usually taken less seriously at puppy shows, where the chief objective is to thank the puppy walkers for playing a valuable role in the development of young foxhounds, although there is always a smattering of guests around the ring who are genuinely interested in the judging. The Duke of Beaufort's puppy show at Badminton, which is attended by hound breeders and masters from around the country, is a notable exception to this generalisation, together with a handful of other influential kennels. It is unusual to attend a puppy show where the importance of puppy walkers is not referenced, and it is no coincidence that the best walks consistently produce hounds who go on to cut the mustard out hunting, whereas a puppy that is shut up or neglected at walk may never make the grade at all.

The head start afforded to a puppy well walked cannot be overstated, and it should be a golden rule of every kennel that no one should be prevailed upon to walk puppies unless they genuinely want to do so. The puppy show is also a day for the hunt staff, who will have been working hard all spring and summer to ensure that the kennels and stables look at their immaculate best. Hounds that show themselves confidently and well are a tribute to the many hours their kennel huntsman will have spent practising and preparing for his biggest day of the year. He will also have played a part in nominating the best working hounds from the previous season, who is usually brought into the ring immediately after the judging for everyone to admire. When the cups and prizes are dispensed after tea, the silverware for the prestigious best worker is invariably the largest of them all, and the cup every puppy walker would most like to win.

An invitation to judge another hunt's puppy show is a privilege that I have never turned down, for it offers a fascinating insight into how other hunts work and the type of hound they are breeding. No two formats for the day are exactly the same, but having selected their two judges, most masters invite them to a sumptuous summer lunch beforehand. Some hunts, such as the Meynell under Johnny Greenall's mastership, and the much smaller Goathland when Graham Pickering was in charge, welcome all comers to a generous spread inside a large marquee, while others host a smaller and more exclusive gathering. I was thrilled when joining Lord Yarborough's small party for lunch at Brocklesby Park to find myself sitting opposite Stubbs' iconic and famous 1792 painting of Brocklesby Ringwood, whose descendants I was shortly about to inspect in the ring.

After judging the Blackmore and Sparkford Vale, it was a delight to be taken by Rupert Nuttall to inspect Yarcombe covert, which his farm overlooked. As a child, I devoured Charles Willoughby's superb book, *Come and Hunt*, which features an evocative Peter Biegel painting of hounds streaming away from the same covert at the start of a good hunt. Duncan Sharp and his wife, Pat, may not have owned a famous painting or fox covert, but lunch at their lovely home of great antiquity prior to the Rockwood Harriers puppy show was one of the best I've ever had. The Rockwood Chairman played football as a professional for Barnsley before taking up hunting and building a successful haulage business, and I recall his generous hospitality whenever I see Rockwood hounds on the flags, albeit the pack was absent from Harrogate when Charles Frampton and I judged the harriers there in 2016.

The young entry are usually judged at the kennels, but this is by no means set in stone; for many years Captain Wallace chose to hold his puppy show at a supporter's farm. The doghound puppies are always shown first for obvious reasons, but it is unusual to see the young entry brought into the ring together at the start of both dog and bitch judging. This is a pity, for the judges' task is made so much easier if they are given an opportunity to appraise the standard of entry before starting, as is the case at Badminton, Chipping Norton and Broadway. When the entry is large, experienced judges sometimes ask the kennel huntsman to stand by the gate where they can quickly weed out several that have no chance of making the grade. The owner of a stallion hound responsible for several of the puppies on show is often one of the judges, in which case his co-judge may have to work hard to ensure there is no bias.

After the judging has been completed, there are speeches and tea to follow, but not necessarily in that order. The judges at every puppy show I organised were always asked to make an address before leaving the ring, which avoided the embarrassment of a much-reduced crowd an hour or so later. The accepted protocol is that the senior judge speaks first, and that hunt staff are not put through the ordeal, although many are very happy to do so. The best speakers are confident, interesting and complimentary with just the right sort of joke to end up with. Some restraint may be necessary in the joke department; a French hunting friend of mine was not at all amused by a judge's denouncement of his race during the speeches at Birdsall one year. I've listened to only one toe-curlingly awful puppy show speech, which was a twenty-minute sycophantic ramble that left most of us gasping for air when it was finally done.

Formalities draw to a close after the older hounds have been produced for inspection following tea, after which most kennel huntsmen welcome all survivors into their house for a farewell drink that can last into the small hours – that was certainly the case at the Rockwood's lively party, where their long-suffering professional huntsman, Clive Richardson, eventually called time shortly before dawn. Visitors to the South Pembrokeshire Hunt puppy show are treated to tea on the lawn in front of the decayingly elegant Cresselly House, but at some stage the party inevitably shifts downhill to the pub owned by Hugh Harrison-Allen at Cresswell Quay, where the walls are adorned with photographs of hunting, cricketing and racing. Former landlord, Maurice Cole, has pulled his last pint in a pub where he only ever served beer, spirits and pickled eggs. Most of all, the chance to enjoy another hunt's puppy show is a soothing immersion in the finest and most genuine of English hospitality, affording an afternoon amongst men and women who love both the foxhound and hunting.

CHAPTER 20

A hunting competition at Birdsall

There has always been an element that disapproves of showing hounds, claiming that their own pack is bred purely for work. This somewhat naive rationale fails to take into account that hounds are assessed on conformation, not beauty as such, and that a hound with good conformation is destined for a longer and more productive life than one burdened with even the smallest physical defect. It is also no coincidence that the hounds that succeed on the flags usually come from packs that show the best sport in winter.

Competitions where hounds are evaluated on hunting ability rather than on conformation have for long been a feature of hunting with hounds in the USA, but such contests had never been replicated in the UK until Frank Houghton-Brown, with encouragement from Lord Daresbury (the then recently appointed Chairman of the MFHA), organised a unique event in October 1999 that was written up by Rory Knight Bruce for *Horse & Hound* magazine. With the support and permission of the Middleton Hunt Chairman, Michael Willoughby, the expansive Birdsall estate was selected as the setting for a hunting competition open to six invited packs of hounds. The Belvoir and Wynnstay represented old English blood; the College Valley flew the flag for northern hill hounds, and the David Davies represented the Welsh. Modern English hounds were showcased by the Quorn and the Middleton host pack. Each hunt was asked to bring three couple of their best hounds, with the proviso that they included at least a couple of doghounds, and that every entrant would hunt on both days of the competition so as to make it a true test of stamina.

Frank asked me to chair a panel of judges that included the mounted huntsmen of all six packs together with Colonel Nick Crossley and Alastair Jackson on foot. Every hound was identified by a different number sprayed clearly on its flank, and it was decided that each judge would be allowed to award up to ten points whenever a hound impressed, but were not permitted to score their own hounds. Points were to be awarded at the judge's discretion for attributes such as voice, drive, accuracy, fox finding and recovering the line at a check, but could also be deducted for misdemeanours such as skirting, babbling or running mute. There cannot be a better setting in which to stage a competition of this nature than Birdsall, where low-lying arable and parkland surrounding the big house climb steeply by way of a wide, rugged and grassy escarpment to the very top of the Yorkshire wolds. Furthermore, much of the open and accessible estate offers commanding views across a wild and well-foxed landscape that has always been a delight to hunt across. Frank led the joint pack, followed by a field of more than seventy riders from the Birdsall kennels at 9 a.m. on the first day, and soon afterwards Anthony Nicholson viewed a fox away from the Pits. Scent was difficult, but hounds hunted nicely across to Mount Ferrant during a hunt in which the sixth season David Davies woolly doghound, Benjamin '94, was particularly prominent.

The judges had been encouraged to ride as close to the action as possible in order to identify the best hounds, and we had ample opportunity to do just that during a fine two-hour run on a fox from Leys Wood. Middleton Acklam '96 was seldom out of the action and reinforced her contribution to the hunt with a lovely, deep voice throughout; by the time Frank blew for home at 2.15 p.m. she had amassed twenty-three points and built up an unassailable lead ahead of Wynnstay Paragon '95 and the elderly Benjamin. The hunting had rarely been fast on what was only a moderate scenting day, but the judges had been able to observe hounds at close quarters during a morning that favoured the line hunters and older, cold-scenting entrants.

Lord and Lady Halifax entertained visiting masters, judges and hangers-on at a typically lively and generous party at their shooting lodge in Givendale that evening, after which the master of the Wynnstay was seen leaving with the blonde daughter of another Welsh MFH. Our heads the following morning were perhaps not quite as clear as the glorious autumnal sunshine awaiting us at Birdsall for the second consecutive day, during which the Belvoir professional huntsman, Martin Thornton, hunted hounds. In Richard Carden, Joss Hanbury and Rad Thomas, the field included three of my Quorn joint masters, together with many other visitors from around the country, although sadly not the Cattistock who had intended bringing some of their American cross hounds, but had to pull out due to the cough. Martin had the pack smartly away on a fox found above Birdsall Grange, which was run to ground and killed in Cayburn Wood – he took the brush of a fox, which, as Rory pointed out in his article, was the first in British history to be killed by six packs of hounds.

They later hunted with great perseverance and cry all around Mount Ferrant, culminating in a pretty circular hunt in the open that was eventually reduced to walking pace, which enabled even closer scrutiny of individual hounds at work. In contrast to the previous day when the eldest hounds had taken the limelight, it was the turn of hounds with the energy of youth to sparkle on the second day, and it gave me huge pleasure to watch our second-season bitch, Quorn Banish '98, cutting out the work to such good effect that she accumulated enough points to earn second place in the bitch class behind Middleton Acklam. The College Valley's Gosling '95 beat Benjamin by just one point in the doghound category while third places in each class were filled by the Wynnstay and Belvoir, meaning that hounds from all six packs had impressed the judges during a fascinating competition that has sadly never been repeated.

Fittingly, the award for the best pack overall went to the generous Middleton Hunt, which in so many different ways had been the perfect hosts. During breakfast held in a big marquee at the Birdsall kennels at the end of the second day, everyone agreed on how remarkably well the pack of six hunts had welded together to hunt as one unit; above all else, the competition had demonstrated the versatility of the foxhound, and that no particular blood, be it old English, hill hound, Welsh or modern, could claim clear supremacy. News of the competition even crossed the Atlantic, for in due course I received a charming and unexpected letter on the subject from the Iroquois MFH, Jerry Miller.

CHAPTER 21

New life and hunting correspondent during the pre-ban years

By the time the harvest had been gathered in southern England, we had moved to a house not far from Cirencester in the middle of my old VWH stamping ground, where I was to remain for the next couple of years before an eventual return to the Yorkshire farmhouse I had bought during my last season with the Sinnington. In this setting I established a travel company called Wild and Exotic that is still going to this day, which required me to undertake exploratory journeys on horseback across some of the wildest and most beautiful regions of Africa, India, Kyrgyzstan, Mongolia, and South America. On 16 September 2004 I was in a lorry with a group of lady clients trundling into the city of Bayan

Olgii, having watched eagles hunting foxes in the snow-capped Altai Mountains of western Mongolia, when we suddenly came in range of a telephone mast and everyone's mobile started bleeping furiously. In this way and in that strange land, news reached us that eight passionate supporters of hunting had against all odds breached stringent security measures to storm the Houses of Parliament whilst MPs were debating Labour's invidious bill to ban hunting with dogs.

I caught fish such as Indian mahseer, Zambezi tiger fish and tropical golden dorado that I had only ever dreamt about, and enjoyed exciting trips with clients to target Atlantic salmon in Russia and saltwater species in the Caribbean Sea and Indian Ocean. Those many and varied adventures together with some of the extraordinary characters I met along the way do not concern hunting, but are perhaps worthy of another book one day. Immersion in a new life and a young business eased the dull ache of no longer hunting hounds, however, I could not resist taking a look at the Beaufort on my feet in early September, and will never forget the kindness shown by Ian Farquhar, who promptly insisted that I ride a horse of his at Swangrove the following week.

I duly arrived at Badminton to renew acquaintanceship with Kanga, a horse I had tried out hunting during my first season with the Quorn; it had buried me in a ditch. The story of how the 5th Duke of Beaufort enjoyed an exceptional run on a fox from Silk Wood in 1762 and the subsequent conversion of his stag hounds to that quarry is well documented, and lends weight to the claim that Badminton is truly the spiritual home of foxhunting. It certainly felt that way as we hacked through the park across springy turf and past the magnificent herd of resident red deer with the famous stately home and lake gleaming as a backdrop beneath the rising sun. Hounds ran well on foxes from Swangrove, Bodkin Hazel and the Withy Beds, and at the end of the morning distinguished themselves by hunting accurately through a large field of stinking and recently desiccated potatoes.

Following Ian's kindness, others came forward to offer me horses to ride. The first proper day's hunting I had after thirteen seasons as an MFH was a November Saturday with the man who had blooded me when I was just ten years old; that Sidney Bailey was still hunting the same pack of hounds all those years later put things quietly in perspective. Richard Sumner, who had found a home for one of my best Quorn horses in May, lent me one of his own for a particularly well-foxed Heythrop Saturday at Eastington. Despite the abundance of foxes, the field waited patiently for twenty minutes for one to bolt, only for the huntsman to decline to hunt it because it was heading in the wrong direction. Later in the day Richard led the field over an enormous wall whilst hounds were breaking up a fox; five minutes later Anthony Adams trotted through an open gateway 50 yards further down chuckling quietly to himself. Thanks to generous invitations from

Tom Yandle, Robin Smith-Ryland, Martin Gibson and Julian Llewellen Palmer, I also enjoyed days with the Devon & Somerset staghounds, and the Eglington, North Cotswold and Warwickshire hounds that winter.

I was back hunting with the Beaufort in January on a horse called Andy who none of the hunt staff were keen to ride. The gelding had a strange habit of running out at a fence when some way off, but would attack with gusto any obstacle that he could be persuaded to approach within a few strides. We had a four-mile point in the morning, and I had seen enough to compare in my hunting diary that evening the 'think big' mentality of the Beaufort amateur huntsman with the 'play safe' attitude of some other exponents I had hunted with that season. I rode Andy again in February, when he surprised me by jumping a large hedge from five strides out after Simon Tomlinson had asked me to inspect the electric wire in front of the fence. With the bit between his teeth, Andy flew the next wired up hunt jump and executed a foot-perfect in and out over a road crossing, only to blot his copybook by refusing to approach within a hundred yards of an inviting stone wall. None of us knew it at the time, but by nightfall an outbreak of foot-and-mouth had been confirmed in Essex, which was traced a few days later to Heddon-on-the-Wall in Northumberland. All hunting was immediately suspended, and was not to reappear in the British countryside for ten long and miserable months.

In the meantime I had rediscovered a love of writing – English had been my favourite and only successful subject at school – and I had written intermittently on hunting for Julie Spencer's *Country Illustrated* magazine, which had flourished for a few years in the nineties. Now I was keen to do more, and was commissioned to write several articles for the *Daily Telegraph*, as well as write up interviews with Richard Meade and Arnaud Bamberger, the Managing Director of Cartier, for *The Field* magazine and pen other features for *Country Life*. There was universal relief when a resumption of hunting under strict security measures was announced in December 2001, and for me a telephone call from *The Field*'s features editor, Lucy Higginson, asking whether I could write up the VWH's first day back on Monday, 17 December, and file copy by 10 a.m. the following morning. A call to Christine Mason secured a horse, and in this way I began a part-time career as a hunting correspondent that has endured to this day.

Many of us had found the autumnal English landscape of golden stubbles, grasslands run to seed and trees turning gold much diminished, knowing there was no prospect of hounds making the open spaces and woodlands ring to their cry, but that was all dispelled within minutes of Sidney Bailey throwing hounds in to draw Wellfield Plantation on the edge of Cirencester Park shortly after 9 a.m. The covert was teeming with foxes, and within the hour Sidney was blowing the kill to announce the death of what was possibly the first fox caught by a pack of hounds that season. For everyone out hunting that morning it was as if a dark cloud had been lifted from their lives, for none more so than the VWH huntsman who, in his thirty-fifth season hunting their hounds, was grinning from ear to ear throughout the morning.

The following March I rode a lovely ex-chaser behind a joint meet of the Royal Artillery and South & West Wilts hounds neat Chitterne on the edge of Salisbury Plain on my first assignment for *Horse & Hound* magazine. The meet was held at a charmingly scruffy smallholding where hosts Tony and Marilyn Wood laid on a delicious barbecue breakfast with gallons of cider to wash it down, with an accordionist on hand to add lustre to the carnival atmosphere of a late-season meet. Andrew Sallis hunted hounds for the first half of a busy day beneath skies alive with singing skylarks and wheeling buzzards before handing over to Lt Colonel Nick Foster. We finished within sight of the grey outline of Imber church, having killed a brace on top, its grey silhouette framed between steep slopes of yellow gorse and the distant landmark of Imber Clump. It was amongst these open, rolling hills that Sidney had blooded me as a ten-year-old schoolboy, but the landscape was just as I remembered from nearly thirty years earlier.

Years ago the reputation of an individual hunt could be made or broken by a critical review in the sporting press, and I remember as a child the palpable excitement of an impending *Horse & Hound* visit, but the emphasis has gradually shifted to being a general overview, albeit one hung on the peg of a day's sport. In other words, it was up to the writer to accentuate the positive, and pay as much attention to the diverse cross-section of followers as to the hounds and the country they ran across. I returned from a six-week working visit to Africa at the start of the 2002–03 season to several commissions from the *Horse & Hound* hunting editor, Nicola Swinney, and enjoyed the privileged insight granted by individual hunts to a *Horse & Hound* reporter. I had sold or given away all six of my fine horses when giving up the Quorn, so was entirely reliant on being lent horses to do the job; in the seventeen years I have been writing as a hunting correspondent I have never been asked to ride a really bad one, and only once was expected to pay for a hireling. Nearly every horse was the better side of good, and some, such as the two provided by Peter Daresbury when I visited the Wynnstay, were quite exceptional conveyances.

I was frequently surprised. For example, some hunts were seriously restricted due to shooting interests in a way that was unthinkable in the Sinnington or Quorn countries, although it was always a pleasure to come across a situation of both sports working together. This was the case when I hunted with the Saltersgate Farmers from Cropton and a shooting party greeted us warmly on the way to the first draw. I was surprised when hunting with the Badsworth to discover that we were restricted to a single estate for the entire day, and to see release pens in coverts belonging to the Oakley Hunt, but that did not stop huntsman Paul Bellamy from conjuring up a nice evening hunt. I was interested to meet Mrs Harris at the Melchbourne meet, for one of her daughters had eloped with a neighbouring professional whilst master of the Fitzwilliam and later put down her roots in the Sinnington country, where I soon came to know her as a potential troublemaker. 'Jump on my daughter if you see her', joked Mrs Harris in reference to another daughter who was out that day. I was glad not to have done so, for the lady concerned invited us all in for a fine hunting tea at the end of the day.

Having had more than my share of galloping and jumping across country at the Quorn, it was a pleasure to renew my love of moorland hunting, no matter how big or small the hunt. They don't come much smaller than the tiny Glaisdale in North Yorkshire, where I rode Nick Wykes's fine horse on a bitterly cold day from a meet at Danby Beacon. Master and huntsman, Joe Tindall, wore wellie boots, leggings and waterproofs and rode a fat, fell-type pony. Joe's small but select field included both agent and head keeper's wives to encapsulate an era of hunting on the North York Moors that has since vanished beneath the intensification of driven grouse shooting. His sixteen couple of hill hounds found a fox beside Scaling Dam and hunted well into the teeth of a fresh easterly straight off the grey North Sea. A more genuine or likeable hunt would be hard to find.

Despite being run on a shoestring – the huntsman shod his conveyance with shoes wrenched from dead horses at the local knacker's yard – the Farndale Hunt had been showing superb sport throughout my mastership of the neighbouring Sinnington. I followed them in the dale from which the hunt takes its name, where head keeper Frank Croft had a fine show of foxes in the Bracken Banks. In his book, *The Innocent Eye*, Herbert Read writes of the 'strange, dark and beautiful' race that inhabits the North Yorks Moors, and although no longer cut off from the outside world, many followers that day spoke in a language that outsiders would struggle to comprehend; words such as *shoaly*, *wheezed* and *gleesey* regularly cropped up in conversation. Shoaly was the nickname given to their huntsman, Bryan Marshall, who much preferred his feet to riding, and the word was derived from the verb shoal or fall, as in 'to shoal off his horse'.

Equally fascinating was an opportunity to observe the Exmoor hounds in the post-Wallace era on behalf of *Country Life* magazine. Having given up the Heythrop in 1977, the Captain had hunted the Stars of the West for twenty-five successful seasons, and drawn visitors from all over the world to hunt in landscape that the artist Cecil Aldin referred to as the riding playground of England. I had enjoyed several days with the Exmoor over the years and admired the high standard of hound they used to exhibit at Peterborough and Honiton, although their huntsman, Tony Wright, never looked as if he was entirely happy in the show ring. He handled hounds with quiet and sympathetic concentration on the hunting field and we enjoyed a busy August morning amidst the lovely Barle valley, where the sole master, Felicita Busby, kept the field well in touch. Ronnie had recruited Felicita to his mastership nine years earlier and she is still at the head of affairs nearly a quarter of a century later. After the morning was over, I visited the Captain's grave, which stands in a quiet corner of a moorland churchyard, which foxes are said to cross regularly.

It was a privilege to write up one of the last days of another hunting legend in the far north, where Martin Letts was stepping down from hunting the College Valley & North Northumberland after thirty-nine seasons and it was something of a challenge to do the renowned hound man justice in print. His celebrated hill hounds, which are now owned by Martin's daughter, Diana, caught their fox after a blisteringly fast seventy-minute run over wild and broken country. Fittingly, both Diana and Martin's wife, Eildon, who is named after the nearby range of border hills, were both on hand at the finish. Martin is not known for gratuitous pleasantries on or off the hunting field, and it was reassuring to observe his legendary grumpiness at close quarters when handing out what appeared to be an entirely unnecessary rocket to the hapless field master. During my stay with the Letts family at Hethpool, which is hidden within the folds of giant hills overlooking the College Valley, Martin lamented as his greatest sorrow the decline of the fox from revered quarry species to lowly vermin. He has since written a book summarising a lifetime with hounds; get hold of a copy if you can, for the book is a hunting gem.

It was also a pleasure to see my former amateur whipper-in, Richard Tyacke, showing excellent sport at the adjacent Tynedale during the early years of what has become a glittering huntsman's career; in the shape of things to come, his field were dressed entirely in black or tweed coats. A highlight of my day with the Zetland further south was watching the Lowther Show champion bitch, Crumble '00, cutting out the work after their huntsman, David Jukes, pointed out that she had a line to Border Clasher via my old friend, Sinnington Crofter '95. After my day with the Hurworth in their bicentenary year huntsman Joe Townsend showed me a two hundred-year-old print of hounds and hunt staff gathered beneath an oak tree that is still standing to this day. Whilst out with the Braes of Derwent in County Durham, we rode past an eighteenth-century mansion called Hamsterley Hall where a previous owner, Robert Smith Surtees, wrote his famous works of hunting literature such as *Handley Cross* and *Mr Sponge's Sporting Tour*; I was told that the current owners maintain a link with hunting by walking hound puppies.

Sometimes these visits threw up little gems of interest that were just a little bit too close to the bone to make it into print. In 2003 I attended the Grove and Rufford's Opening Meet at Caunton, where I met Lady Anne Bentinck, who had established a private pack of harriers to hunt her vast Welbeck estate in Nottinghamshire following a disagreement with her local hunt. I was pleased to learn that the Grove & Rufford were once more welcome at Welbeck after joint master Jim Ratcliffe had asked Lady Anne to reconsider. 'Why should I?', she had asked, to which the MFH replied: 'Why not?'. We went on to enjoy a busy day in near-dustbowl conditions behind Roderick Duncan, who was one of the first huntsmen to wear a chin strap on account of a dreadful fall.

When staying with the Vesteys at Little Thurlow Hall to report on the Thurlow's opening meet, my eye was drawn to a handsome silver cup on the mantelpiece, which had been won by the hunt's entry for the last *Hunting* magazine and MFHA conservation competition ever held. The cup had originally been awarded to the champion doghound at Peterborough and presumably won outright by the Warwickshire Hunt many years earlier. As Lord Willoughby de Broke was both Chairman and a director of the magazine, and given his family's long-standing connection with the Warwickshire, it was easy to piece together the pieces of that particular jigsaw. After hounds had been blessed at the meet the following day, I was able to observe at first-hand the conservation benefits of an all-round sporting estate where hunting and shooting flourished in tandem. Edmund Vestey, who was Chairman of the MFHA from 1992 to 1996, was in his thirtieth season carrying the horn, initially with the Puckeridge & Thurlow, but since 1985 with the separated Thurlow Hunt.

During Edmund's tenure as Chairman, the Countryside Movement commissioned the Phelps report, a 1997 review of hunting with hounds that now gathers dust at the Museum of English Rural Life in Reading. I served on the MFHA sub-committee formed to address the recommendations of the report, which resulted in several complicated changes to rules on terrier work designed to appease our opponents. In retrospect, rules that permitted the bolting of foxes from some sanctuaries but not from others, and distinguished between foxes that were fresh and hunted were unnecessarily restrictive and ambiguous. Many masters struggled to interpret them accurately, and although well intentioned, the new rules only added to a huntsman's woes. If practitioners failed to grasp the complexities, it is safe to assume that the changes were neither understood nor appreciated by our opponents. For me and other huntsmen, the new rules introduced at the start of the 1998 season became just another stick to beat us with, and I regret my own lack of foresight when serving on the committee.

The Thurlow could not quite be described as a private pack; however, that was very much the title claimed by the Staffordshire Moorland, whose hounds were kennelled on Johnny Greenall's Derbyshire estate under the supervision of former Meynell huntsman, David Barker, whose wife hunted the hounds. I joined them for a lovely all grassland day in the picturesque Manifold valley, where the hunt was accorded a friendly reception by many of the walkers we encountered on the banks of the River Dove. Elaine showed that she was just as capable at hunting hounds as the men, dispensing a rocket to anyone who got in her way. Early the same season I reported an atmosphere of resilience and hope for *Horse & Hound* when hunting with the York and Ainsty South on their newcomers' day, when more than twenty riders enjoyed their first day's hunting in relentless rain. I pointed out that the hunt's commitment to the future was being mirrored across the country by others, not only by encouraging new recruits, but also by continuing to breed hounds, nurture their hunting countries and establish new coverts.

Despite such commitment to the future, the sense of euphoria that had enveloped the hunting world following the successes of protests culminating in the 2002 Liberty and Livelihood March in central London was gradually draining away as it became increasingly clear that the Labour government had no intention of listening to the four hundred thousand people who had travelled from all over Britain and beyond to take part. Thousands had arrived in the capital under their own steam, but others came into London on thirty-one specially chartered trains and 2,500 coaches to participate in a demonstration that was the largest of its kind in British history. The event grabbed front page headlines around the world and was generally well received by an incredulous press; in attempting to explain the size of the protest, one reporter invited his readers to imagine an FA Cup final crowd walking down Whitehall every hour, for hours on end.

The triumphant atmosphere of defiance that enveloped the Hyde Park Rally seemed a very long time ago on 17 November 2004 when I rode behind Ian Farquhar and his Beaufort bitches from a sombre meet at the kennels the morning after the Parliament Act had been invoked to allow the House of Commons to overrule the Lords and put in place a ban on hunting with dogs that was to come into force on 18 February 2005. In this way a tradition going back hundreds of years was thought to have been extinguished by a legislative device that had been deployed on only six previous occasions since its inception ninety-three years earlier. The previous evening I had nearly been catapulted through the window of Ian's car when he slammed on the brakes to avoid running over a fox on the way out to dinner, but the irony of his reaction would have been beyond the comprehension of nasty backbenchers such as Tony Banks and Gerald Kaufman who had pushed so hard for the ban.

There was a sense of disbelief amongst the huge mounted field assembled at Badminton the following morning, most of them dressed in the hunt's smart blue and buff livery, but also a quiet determination to find a way through the mess ahead, which was reflected in Ian's carefully worded address before hounds moved off. The large crowd roared in appreciation and gratitude after he assured them that there will always be hounds and hunting at Badminton, even if he was not yet sure just how that could be achieved. Many of those present had already signed a declaration of intent to break the law and continue hunting after the ban, and the elderly Duke of Devonshire had told me in an interview for *The Field* magazine that he fully intended joining them in prison if necessary.

In the fullness of time it was to become clear that nobody would be going to prison for contravening the Hunting Act, and that the full weight of responsibility lay with masters and hunt staff rather than subscribers and followers; but no one knew that in November 2004 and my day with the Beaufort was tinged with uncertainty and just a little fear. And just a little optimism too, for at dinner the previous evening I had been told to look out for farmers' sons Charlie Dando and Rory Akerman, as young faces of the future, so knew the muddy boy who rode up to introduce himself following a fall must be one of them. During our conversation it was quickly established that the twelve-year-old would take over carrying the horn should the Captain be incarcerated in jail, and that Rory would make a suitable whipper-in.

As the February day when the ban was due to become law drew ever closer, many were determined to make the most of what precious time they believed was left before a rural way of life was consigned to the history books. Amongst others there existed a sense of disbelief that a longstanding and respected institution in the English countryside could ever be destroyed by those who had little or no knowledge of its customs, traditions and practices. That was very much the case amongst followers of the South Durham Hunt when I joined them for a meet at the Black Bull in Trimdon, a Labour heartland at the centre of Tony Blair's constituency, just weeks before the ban was to become law. The landlord was proud of the fact that Mr Blair had used his pub as a watering hole and told me that the Prime Minister had better things to worry about than foxes.

The master, Mark Shotton, pointed out the Blairs' red brick house on the way to the meet and explained how difficult it was for local people to reconcile their support for Labour with the party's hatred of hunting. Like many others I met that day, he did not think that the Prime Minister had particularly strong views on hunting, just that he cared much more about appeasing backbenchers in return for their support over the war in Iraq. As if to underline their determination to keep going, Simon Dobinson and the South Durham hounds produced a four-mile point against a drab background of collieries, spoil heaps and rough, grassy hills. They travelled faster than any pack I had hunted with that season, but sadly not behind 'Tony Blair's fox', which was often found in a thorn covert next to the Prime Minister's house.

In the run up to the ban, Jonathan Young, editor of *The Field* magazine, asked me to report on a day's drag hunting with the Berks and Bucks drag hounds, whose master, Ian Balding, kindly provided a horse for me to ride from a meet at Bucklebury. The horse was a good one, we jumped lots of fences and everyone was most welcoming, but nothing could compensate for the lack of venery and unpredictability of the genuine chase. I was reminded of my summer visits to judge hounds in Germany, where I once rode on a short hunt and discovered that drag hunting was little more than an exclusive club of wealthy horse owners. What the club lacked was the deeper involvement of the rural community, so many of whom turn out in cars and on foot throughout an English winter to watch a carefully bred pack of hounds pursuing a wild quarry across a familiar landscape. To catch a fleeting glimpse of a fox is the icing on their cake, and when asked whether they have had a good day, many car followers will simply respond by revealing how many different foxes they have seen.

I joined the Bedale at the Green Dragon pub at Exelby twenty-four hours before the ban on hunting became law for what I assumed would be the last day's hunting as I had known it all my life. Ironically, the hunt was being welcomed back to a venue they had not met at for at least fifty years. Charles Frampton and his hounds worked hard to find foxes on the shooting estates of Thorpe Perrow and Clifton, and caught one in the parkland surrounding Clifton Castle before home was blown at dusk to conclude a busy day. My thoughts as we waited for the hunt lorry to appear in failing light were for the hounds clustered in a steaming jumble of tired and happy bodies, for they knew nothing of the uncertainty that lay ahead. There was to be no reporting during the first few weeks of the ban, and two days later I flew to Buenos Aires on business. On arrival I checked my emails at the Claridge hotel, and a friend's one-liner leapt up from the screen and hit me between the eyes. 'Good hunt today', it read. 'Killed a brace on top.' Clearly, and despite the best intentions of their huntsmen, it was going to take time for hounds to learn the new law of the land.

CHAPTER 22

Post-ban years

Some hunts decided to end their season earlier than usual in 2005; others experimented with laying false lines for the first time or endeavoured to continue hunting within the framework of the new law. As had been the case with Trevor Adams and the Duke of Buccleuch's Hunt in Scotland three years earlier, a handful of brave hunts and their masters came forward to challenge legislation and maintain as many traditions, standards and practices as legally permissible. That summer I met the *Horse & Hound* editor, Lucy Higginson, Nigel Peel and one or two others for a working lunch in London, during which we discussed the challenges of reporting on hunting going forward; happily it was agreed that hunting reports would continue in the famous equestrian magazine, and in due course contributors came to realise that there are few impediments to accurately describing post-ban hunting in print.

I was back from Argentina in time to write up Sidney Bailey's last day carrying the horn in Cirencester Park on 26 March. Over three hundred mounted followers and more than a thousand on foot turned up to say goodbye to the consummate professional, who had hunted the same pack for a remarkable forty-three years, which amounted to more than five thousand days in the saddle as a huntsman. Hunt staff and masters from near and far formed a colourful guard of honour for Sidney and his hounds to pass through on their way to the meet at Ten Rides. During the day's sport Christine Mason told me that just ten or fifteen riders turned out for the first few days after the ban, but that within a few weeks normal numbers had returned to the hunting field. With hounds loaded up after a busy day, VWH senior master, Mark Hill, removed his hunting cap and called for three resounding cheers in honour of the man he had hunted with throughout his life.

The restrictions on hunting in Scotland had become law back in 2002, and everyone closely connected with the sport was aware that Trevor Adams had successfully established the principle of using a full pack of hounds to flush foxes to guns, which was not legally permitted south of the border. Trevor's interpretation of the law was vindicated when an attempt to prosecute him for illegal hunting was thrown out of court, which gave much comfort to other Scottish hunts unsure of the best way forward. The Bicester with Whaddon Chase travelled north with Patrick Martin in the autumn of 2005 to hunt the College Valley and Duke of Buccleuch countries by invitation and enjoy the freedom of legal pursuit with a full complement of hounds, although in my subsequent report for *Horse & Hound* I referred to the unpalatable spectre of foxes being gunned down in the hunting field.

The Hunting Act allowed only two hounds to be deployed to flush the quarry to guns south of the border, which offered little assistance for hunts to provide effective fox control but was found to be a useful exemption for the three West Country packs of staghounds hunting a much stronger scenting quarry. The Devon and Somerset were determined to continue managing Exmoor's herd of wild red deer, and to do so within the law even if that meant hunting in relays using just two hounds at any one time. The hunt had been dealt a bitter blow by the National Trust's ban on staghunting eight years earlier, which was imposed following the Bateson report and shut down deer hunting on the 12,000-acre Holnicote estate, which had been donated to the National Trust by Sir Richard Acland in 1944. I wonder if any of those responsible for this decision had ever seen the charming Lionel Edwards' painting, *Eighteenth Century Stables at Holnicote*. The Trust's shameful imposition of a ban disregarded the requests of their benefactor, who had taken the precaution of listing the continuation of staghunting in his memorandum of wishes. Unfortunately these were not legally binding, and the Trust chose to ignore the specific request of a large donor. The staghounds duly complied with the ruling, although some felt that its defiance would have exposed the National Trust's high-handed arrogance to a wider audience, and possibly led to an overturn of the ban.

A commission from *The Field* to report on how the Devon and Somerset were faring under the new Act was a welcome opportunity to revisit Exmoor after several years, renew friendship with the Yandle family who farm at Riphay Barton, and once more enjoy the generous West Country hospitality of a house that is permanently open to hunting folk. I had first met Tom Yandle when he visited Yorkshire to shoot grouse in the early 1990s; on learning that my Sinnington season was over by the middle of March, he prevailed on me to come down to Exmoor when he was busy lambing and 'keep the hunters going so they don't buck all my guests off at Easter'. I took Tom at his word, and for a number of years enjoyed some superb spring staghunting, riding on possibly the best and most experienced horses on all Exmoor. Tom's middle-aged father had met his upcountry young bride when she came to stay at the Carnarvon Arms with her father, Colonel Heath, and siblings for spring hunting in 1934. Ernest Yandle, who was from a farming and hunting dynasty closely involved with the Tiverton Staghounds, followed the barmaid's advice by selecting the eldest of the three daughters as his future wife, leaving the youngest free to eventually marry Norman Harding, and in the fullness of time become a long-serving master of the Devon and Somerset.

Tom was an all-round sportsman of the old school, as adept at catching salmon on his stretches of the Rivers Barle and Exe as shooting driven grouse in Yorkshire or following hounds in all weathers on tough home-bred horses who skated across the moor whilst others sank in the bogs. His wife, Margaret, had hung up her hunting boots by the time I got to know the Yandle family, but I was an admirer of her practice of taking a spinning rod on the school run whenever there had been a spate on the Exe. Having dropped off the children, she would stop at Chain Bridge on the way home for a couple of upstream casts with a Devon minnow and occasionally returned with a silver salmon in the boot. Having been Chairman of the staghounds since 1996, it fell to her husband to steer the Devon and Somerset through the most challenging period of their 150 year existence, which he achieved with quiet resolve and considerable diplomacy. However, despite the hunt's determination to continue managing Exmoor's herd of wild red deer, the familiar moorland landscape felt strangely empty with just two hounds to fill it, and when writing up the day I compared hunting without hound music to watching a film without sound.

No hunt has yet folded as a consequence of the ban, and it was heartening to report on the Goathland's revival as a popular northern hunt after hitting rock bottom in 2003 when they ceased operating altogether and the country was instead hunted by other invited packs. Local farmer and dedicated hound man,

Graham Pickering, came to the rescue by offering to accommodate hounds at his moorland farm and hunt them twice weekly as a joint master with the local coalman, Richard Cana. The only small problem was that when Graham gave this undertaking there was not a single hound to the hunt's name, but favours were called in from the College Valley, Derwent, Lunesdale, Tynedale and Zetland, all of whom drafted hounds to help form a new pack that included several elderly but low-scenting hounds of great ability. The four-month-old pack provided a superb day's sport on the occasion of my visit, which ended with a fine hunt into the Staintondale country across wild and boggy moorland that would have been the envy of any well-established hunt, let alone one recently back from the dead. In this way the hunt that had been a first pack of hounds for such illustrious amateur huntsmen as Major Gerald Gundry, Colonel Nick Crossley and the North Cotswold's Nigel Peel, was saved and flourishes to this day.

In the immediate aftermath of the ban there had been rumours in the Irish hunting fields of a mass invasion of English visitors, although I found no evidence to support this concern when dispatched across the Irish Sea to investigate by *The Field* magazine. Penny Lindsay-Fynn kindly paved my way for a visit to the Meath, organised a hireling and lent me a black coat for the occasion. In an arrangement that I could not imagine working back in England, hounds were hunted on alternate days by the professional Henry brothers, who took it in turns to act as field master when not carrying the horn. It was Kenny's turn to rule the large field on the day of my visit, which he did with a fist of iron on account of very wet conditions and the multitude of small, grass farms that made up the day's draw. We saw little of hounds at work, and spent a disproportionate amount of time queuing up in single file to jump a succession of yawning dykes. I did not return to England as a convert to Irish hunting, despite the craic afterwards at a local pub where trays of sandwiches were washed down with copious quantities of Guinness. Apart from a brief visit to address the Northern Rangers Hunt Club dinner at Philip and Augusta Shirley's lovely Loch Fea home in County Monaghan, I have not been back since, although I much enjoyed staying with the Harringtons when judging the Irish Hound show at Clonshire with Captain Wallace. I was recently asked to judge the show for a second time at its new Stradbally venue, only for Roddy Bailey to call back two months later and withdraw the invitation in favour of another candidate. 'Don't worry', he said cheerfully, 'we'll get you to do it next year'. He never did.

Other writing assignments included joining the Curre and Llangibby at the historic setting of Itton Court, to whose Norman doors celebrated hound breeders such as Henry Higginson, Ikey Bell and Bill Scott beat a path in the early twentieth century. They came to avail themselves of Welsh cross blood nurtured by Sir Edward Curre that was to have a profound influence on the activity and athleticism of the modern English foxhound. When we trotted past the great man's tombstone with its reference to his famous white hounds, the recent squabbles in Westminster seemed almost inconsequential against a backdrop of such hallowed hunting history. Later in the day the amalgamated hunt's newly appointed master and huntsman, Jacky Thomas, and his hounds made the woodlands ring to music of hound and horn during an exciting afternoon hunt across a trappy, grass country. In my article I recalled a bitch named Dimple by Llangibby Danger (sadly, neither year of entry was given) who dazzled the Pytchley field with her brilliance when loaned to the famous Northamptonshire pack in the late 1880s. An evocative poem describing her influence is to be found in Charles Willoughby's book, *Come and Hunt.*

It was clear during my visit to report on Richard Tyacke hunting the Wynnstay hounds that the atmosphere of this hard-riding hunt in the Welsh borders had been fully restored within nine months of the ban, and that they were determined to continue providing sport of the highest order. As the Wynnstay ushered in the new Tyacke era, so the Burton were busy saying goodnight to Jim Lang, who had been their popular and cheerful huntsman since 1967. My day in Lincolnshire during Jim's final season was full of happy surprises, most significant the discovery of a wild and unspoilt country largely owned by those closely connected to the hunt. During a wide-ranging day we crossed extensive properties owned and farmed by just six different individuals, five of whom were out hunting that day. Joint master Maggie Cracroft-Ely later sent me a postcard of a riderless horse sailing over a hedge to commemorate my fall from the perfectly mannered Kip after a low bough of a tree had neatly removed me from the saddle.

Not all of my assignments were mounted, and it was a pleasure to observe Tom Cranage's quiet and effective handling of the Ampleforth beagles during a superb day in Rosedale on the North York Moors, and to join the Radley beagles for their seventy-fifth anniversary meet in 2016. On returning to the Lake District following a long absence, I was surprised to discover that the Blencathra's huntsman, Barry Todhunter, no longer wore scarlet and that his celebrated fell hounds were often a target for hunt saboteurs. In the far-off days when hundreds of southern visitors used to flock to the fells to enjoys spring hunting on foot each year, the refrain was always that such a pure and unpretentious form of venery would never attract attention from saboteurs. That was clearly the wrong assumption, for Barry has been persistently harried by police and self-styled monitors despite his natural diplomacy and obvious endeavours to work within the law. The same school of thought also applied to the West Country, so deep-rooted were the local inhabitants to the chase. Hunting continues to flourish throughout both Exmoor and the Lake District, but the threat of intrusive surveillance is never far away.

Further to the east I revealed the special delights of another fell-bred pack for *Horse & Hound*, where Catherine Austen was the magazine's new hunting editor. The Liddesdale, who hunt a range of wild and spectacularly beautiful hills in the Scottish borders, were hunted for many years by the laconic and tough Norman Laing, at whose remote farm in the fold of giant hills the pack are kennelled. They are now handled by his son, Angus, from the back of a motorbike, which he rides across country no horse could ever follow. Run as a private pack, the hunt does not publish a meet card, which is just as well because a decision over where to hunt is often taken only a day or two beforehand. The Liddesdale is also the only registered hunt in the MFHA white book that has consistently failed to provide any details for a Chairman. The position does not exist.

A recent morning with the Duke of Beaufort's Hunt was a salutary reminder of hunting's refusal to be suppressed, and that in the prophetic words of the sporting poet Will Ogilvie: 'Good men follow the good men gone'. Hounds are now hunted by the charming and erudite Matt Ramsden, who I remember from Sinnington days as Tom Holt's schoolboy partner in crime at Ravenswick. There was a large turnout for the 7 a.m. meet at Warren's Gorse and hounds moved off with a punctuality that would have impressed the most critical of old-timers. Matt's amateur whipper-in lent me a foot-perfect and mannerly hunter that I would happily have taken home to Yorkshire. His owner was clearly a valued member of the close-knit team the new Beaufort huntsman relies upon for help and advice. It was only much later that I realised that Charlie Dando was the same fresh faced, muddy young boy who had ridden up to introduce himself the day after the ban on hunting had been announced eleven years earlier.

CHAPTER 23

Hunting abroad

Writing assignments occasionally took me much further afield, and it was always heartening to discover hounds of English extraction in different parts of the world. I once met an ancient foxhound sprawled across the threshold of an estancia in Patagonia, and my heart went out to him when he thumped his hairless stern against the dusty hearth in welcome. Having learnt that some Middleton hounds had been drafted to Trinidad, I persuaded the *Daily Telegraph* to commission a feature on hunting on the Caribbean island, where I was welcomed warmly by Bob Severattan and his family. His pack was really a trencher-fed one, for several of Bob's Indian friends kept a couple or two of hounds in their back yard with which to hunt such exotic species as lappe, agouti and small, native deer.

These hounds were nurtured as prized possessions, but the highest regard was reserved for the recent imports from Yorkshire, who had settled in well to their new surroundings and were destined to enjoy a life of hunting and breeding in equal measure. At the time of my visit, Kate Hoey's Middle Way Group was busy drafting proposals for licensed hunting back in the UK, but Trinidad's

1997 Conservation of Wildlife Act had laid down clear regulations for hunting with hounds that members of the Hunters Association of Trinidad and Tobago were happy to comply with. When reading the legislation, I recognised many similarities with the Middle Way proposals, but having been banned, hunting in England remains unregulated by any Act of Parliament.

Hunting on foot in dense rain forest was certainly a novelty; we sweated in thick, rubber boots that were liberally doused with ammonia to repel snakes and carried cutlasses to hack our way through the jungle. After one 5 a.m. start the small pack settled on to the line of a deer and ran so hard that during the latter stages of the hunt the quarry collided with a van parked up beside a road twisting through the jungle. The end came shortly afterwards beneath a clump of banana trees in a smallholder's garden and, after the hounds were loaded up, the carcass was driven back to the Severattans' suburban home on the outskirts of Port of Spain and handed over to the ladies to cook. Only a handful of us had been out hunting early that morning, but within a few hours extended family and friends started to arrive, attracted by the delicious smelling stew that was bubbling away in a huge, steel cauldron in the small backyard. In Trinidad they hunted for food, and wild meat held a special cachet in the hearts of the Indian communities.

In Kenya, my close friend Tristan Voorspuy stepped up to the mark and saved East Africa's last surviving hunt when Ginger Bell left him an entire pack of hounds in his will. Under Tristan's mastership, hounds only ever hunted a drag, and always met at Deloraine, the Voorspuys' elegant colonial mansion on the edge of the Rift Valley near Rongai. The pack was swelled by some drafts sent out by the East Cornwall, which are kennelled close to the home of Lucinda Voorspuy's parents; Cindy also organised an annual hunt ball, which raised enough money to keep the show on the road for twelve months at a time. The following morning several guests rode to hounds at the 7 a.m. meet still wearing dinner jackets from the night before. A hunt was often laid on for guests recuperating at Deloraine after one of Tristan's legendary Offbeat riding safaris, and more than one survivor of Mara river crossings, elephant charges and horse-hungry lions ended up groaning on the deck during a fast, early morning hunt.

After my first Kenyan hunt, Tristan handed me his horn to blow the kill whilst the pack devoured their reward on the banks of a muddy dam. Many years later I was to blow the very same horn beneath a hot, blue sky from a high, rocky ridge in the Masai Mara after family and close friends had scattered Tristan's remains about the gnarled roots of a beautiful fig tree. Always devoid of fear and assured of his own convictions, Tristan had saddled up his favourite white stallion and ridden out to investigate a property burnt down by natives invading his wild and beautiful ranch in Laikipia. Murdered at close range by a madman brandishing an AK-47, Tristan died protecting a landscape he had loved and nurtured for the last twenty years. Riddled with bullets, his horse limped off into the bush and was devoured the same night by lions and hyenas.

Outings with Ian Burr's bobbery pack in the Blue Mountains of New South Wales remain my only experience of hunting in Australia; however, I have been invited back twice to judge the Oakland Hound Show close to Melbourne. The annual show is impeccably organised each October by Randall Cameron-Kennedy, whose family enjoy long and close connections to the Oakland Hunt, and attracts several of the country's thirteen registered mounted packs. Each year an English judge divides the spoils between the host pack and the neighbouring Melbourne, for both hunts have used blood recently imported from the Beaufort and Exmoor to breed hounds of impressive quality and size. On my recent visit the Oakland were shown by their joint master and huntsman, Rupert Inglesant, whose father had been such a help to me in Leicestershire; a few months later Rupert announced that he would be coming home to take up his new appointment as master and huntsman of the Cotswold in Gloucestershire. Stays with the Cameron-Kennedys always include a close look at their unspoilt, rolling, grass hunting country, which appears to be the most delectable landscape imaginable, but I am never quite sure how deeply or enthusiastically the hunt is embraced by the wider rural community.

In March 2008 I was invited to judge a three-week hunting jamboree in the western states of the USA known as the Western Hunt Challenge, where coyote are pursued by hunts beyond the radar of most hound enthusiasts from Britain. I had once enjoyed a day with the Eglinton and Caledon in Canada but had never ridden to hounds in the well-known hunting states of Alabama, Georgia, Maryland, Pennsylvania and Virginia. This competition was a welcome opportunity to experience hunting in the rougher, wilder lands of the west where the cowboy culture and pioneer spirit endure. I was met off the plane in St Louis by my co-judge, the swashbuckling Grosvenor Merle-Smith, who was to be my constant companion for the next three weeks. The Virginian had hunted with me at the Quorn and, thankfully, we gelled at once.

The next day we drove four hundred miles across the state of Missouri to Omaha, passing through a relentlessly frigid landscape of skeletal cotton wood trees, sour yellow plains and grey sheets of glinting floodwater smeared with rafts of geese. Overhead, huge and disparate flocks of migrating sand hill cranes pushed purposefully onwards across leaden skies. A lively evening in the Ameristar hotel in Tusk was followed by a blank and bleak day with the North Hills Hunt that ended with Bloody Marys at the clubhouse and my first meeting with the irrepressible Betty Hollander, who had a brown, weathered face, piercing, blue eyes, snow-white teeth and an accent thick as treacle. Betty was to participate in every hunt, party and breakfast for the entire trip, hauling her two horses three thousand miles across western states in a goose-neck trailer, whereas Grosvenor and I hopped on to an aeroplane whenever the drive looked tough.

Some six hundred miles further west, we were the only guests staying at the Best Western Hotel on the ice-bound streets of Lusk, Wyoming, but that evening we joined some interesting characters from the Knoxville and Arapahoe hunts at the insalubrious surroundings of the Silver Dollar bar. Arapahoe kennel huntsman, Bob Knox, wore a pristine, white stetson above a drooping, steel-grey moustache and a long, hooked nose. When an Indian local started to mock Bob's hat, an old-fashioned bar-room brawl was narrowly averted by the timely intervention of Joe Emile, who had named his own pack of hounds after his hunting hero. The Knoxville hounds and their casually dressed huntsman produced a sparkling thirty-minute hunt on a coyote the following day, which was run to ground high up in the hills. 'Everyone needs a pat on the back', said Joe, when I congratulated him on their performance. There was no fancy clubhouse attached to the Knoxville; instead, we reconvened for tacos and beer at a truck stop where a sign above the door read 'Welcome Hunters' and gaming machines inside offered shots at moose, elk and coyote.

So taken were we with Joe and his Californian girlfriend, who operated a coal excavator for a living, that we checked out of the Best Western and instead spent the night at their smallholding beside the Upper Plate River in Douglas County. Several shots of tequila later, I slept the night on a sofa in Joe's mobile home beneath walls smothered with the stuffed heads of elk, white-tail deer, coyote and fox, and the stretched-out hides of grizzly bears. It transpired that deer were an emotive subject on this farm, for Joe had become incensed after hunters from Michigan acquired a small block of land next to his own and came down in winter to shoot them. After smearing hound shit on tree trunks failed to deter deer from entering his rivals' land, Joe took to loosing off his scatter gun above their heads, which eventually got him arrested. Half a mile beyond a rich alluvial plain where Joe grows alfalfa and plants cover crops for pen-raised pheasants, the land rises steeply in a broken, jagged mess known as the Badlands. We headed straight into those hills early the following morning for an unscheduled hunt on Joe's tough stock horses and ran a coyote for miles into the distance.

We were reacquainted with Bob Knox for a meet of the Arapahoe hounds close to the outskirts of Denver, Colorado, where the master and newly elected President of the American MFHA hunted hounds against a backdrop of the Rocky Mountains. The appointment of Dr Marvin Beeman from a land of cattlemen and cowboys was something of a coup for the west, for as Marvin pointed out, not only was he was the first President to have been selected from west of the Mississippi

River, he was also raised to hunt coyote rather than foxes. For some reason the Arapahoe had not entered the competition, but the predominantly English-bred pack gave a good account of themselves and were impressive at a check. Their quiet and sympathetic huntsman enjoys a fine rapport with the pack he has been closely connected with throughout his life, and at the end of the day dismounted to walk in amongst his hounds and congratulate them on their performance. Not every hunt we visited had a huntsman or hounds of quite the same quality.

However, Paul Delaney's Grand Canyon Hunt in Arizona was equally impressive, and provided the best day's hunting of our visit, during which we never left an enormous 55,000-acre paddock. The mainly Walker hounds were hunted by a dedicated young professional called Peter Wilson, ably supported by Jimmy Boyes as the first whipper-in, happy in Arizona nearly twenty years after leaving the same position at the Quorn in Leicestershire. A thoroughly professional team was completed by Amanda Wilson, whose hat held high signalled a coyote on the move soon after leaving the 9 a.m. meet. During the 7-mile hunt that ensued through a land unblemished by roads, towns or any other impediment to sport, I was able to absorb the challenges of hunting coyote with hounds in the driest and harshest of conditions.

I was mounted on a superlative flea-bitten grey whose long, easy stride devoured the ground and allowed close observation of hounds at work, most of which was achieved by the leading two couple with the others strung out some way behind. There was a palpable sense of relief when a check occurred after a blisteringly fast run on a coyote that seemed quite unperturbed by his pursuit; in such an arid environment it was hardly surprising that hounds were keener to find water than recover the line. The ease with which the quarry outdistanced his pursuers combined with their discomfort in the dry conditions felt just a little unnatural; they had run flat out for most of the hunt, yet still lacked the speed to effect a successful conclusion. I wondered whether an injection of lighter framed fell blood would help, or better still the greyhound's hybrid vigour to even up the odds a little on those wide western plains.

The master, Paul Delaney, had spared no expense when building the Arizona Hunt's state of the art kennels, which were also home to half a dozen jaunty Jack Russells and almost as many lurchers. After enjoying a sumptuous hunt breakfast out in the field, which was served on white tablecloths decorated with fresh flowers, we took the long dogs coursing on the sage-bush plains. The wildlife here must be Teflon-coated, for five lean and ultra-fit lurchers were unable to catch a hare, although we did manage to lamp one at night, which reappeared jugged for a hunt supper the following evening. We also hunted from the base of Paul's comfortable guest house with the Paradise Valley Beagles, who tried their hearts out in the dry heat and included a beagle with Stowe blood coursing through her veins. After this hospitable interlude amongst the most genuine of hunting men and women it was time to visit the remote gold mining outpost of Battle Mountain in Nevada for a rare day off and the chance to hunt mountain lion with the extraordinary Jace and Catherine Albati.

Jace collected us from the Super 8 motel at the crack of dawn and swung his pick-up into the unrelenting slate grey mountains that were to be our playground for the day. Although our quarry was the large mountain lion or cougar, locals such as Jace often refer to them in conversation as cats, which are not to be confused with the much smaller and more numerous bobcat. It would be hard to meet a couple keener on hunting and hounds than the husband and wife team blessed with film-star good looks who maintained three separate packs with which to hunt coyote, mountain lion and bear. Cougar enjoy the full protection of the law in neighbouring California but are still legal game in Nevada during certain months of the year; their pelts are so valuable that several locals set aside conventional work during mid-winter to pursue them for financial gain. In 1981 a trapper from across the border in Idaho was challenged by law-enforcement officials at his remote campsite in the mountains for illegally hunting bobcat and deer. Claude Dallas shot both men dead, tossing one body into a river and dragging the other into a coyote's den before spending fifteen long months on the run. He was eventually captured not far from where we were hunting that day, and served twenty-two years for voluntary manslaughter before his recent release. For some Dallas epitomised the Wild West by defying the government and living off the land; others saw him as a cold-blooded killer who got off lightly following a sensational trial.

Jace explained that a whole week should be set aside for a proper lion hunt, with the initial stages being devoted to finding the quarry with just two hounds, although up to four more are laid on after the quarry has been properly found. Once a hunt has reached this stage, we were told that hounds would never abandon the line, and that chances of success were very high. The Albatis' pack of Walker hounds included a smidgeon of Airedale terrier blood, which no doubt contributed to their willingness to take a cougar on if it were unwise enough not to take refuge amongst the many high, rocky ledges that adorn the mountains. With just one free day at our disposal the odds were stacked against our finding a mountain lion, let alone getting on terms with one, although we were told that machinery or vehicles left beside any of the few tracks snaking through the bleak landscape made for a good place to start; apparently, a Tom cannot resist marking something strange or new with a spray of his urine. 'Lions are curious', Jace told us. 'If you have a house cat, you can figure them out really well'. Having abandoned the pick-up, we climbed steadily uphill into cold, grey mountains daubed with deep spreads of snow whilst the two hounds scoured the slopes for a trail. Each was fitted with a sturdy radio transmitter, which meant that they could continue hunting through the night if necessary, and be safely relocated at daybreak the following morning. The equipment was designed to emit a series of quicker staccato bleeps should the wearer be tilting its head whilst baying furiously at a ledged mountain lion.

The mountains swallowed us up as we yomped up scree slopes and along rocky creek bottoms where trees stood like skeletons and the dead branches beneath lay like bundles of bleached bones. Occasionally we glimpsed an eagle soaring overhead, saw fleeting herds of elegant deer or were momentarily startled by a covey of chukkas erupting from the bare slopes. In the bowels of such a creek an eighth-season bitch pressed her nose into a 3-inch deep print in the snow and gave tongue, which invigorated her companion into action. Unfortunately, the cougar was too far gone for pursuit and the line fizzled out within a few hundred yards, nor was there sufficient snow covering for the wise old bitch to follow the line of prints by eyesight rather than nose, as she had taught herself to do. We scoured the slopes for an obvious path out over the top, for lions favour the easiest route up a mountain. 'Look for where you would ride a horse – that's the place', Jace explained, but it was not to be. We walked off the hills at dusk without having got a hunt, but I had seen and heard enough of the remarkable Walker strain of hound to become a fan.

We stayed in a cramped trailer parked up in the yard of the Red Rock kennels for the last leg of the competition, which was hosted by the inimitable Lynn Lloyd, who put down her roots in Nevada having run out of gas on a journey from the east to the west coast. Having scrimped, saved and given riding lessons for a few months, Lynn was able to acquire a small block of land without down payment, purchase her first Walker hounds and build a small, wooden shack. Through grit and hard work, her original holding was eventually exchanged for a much larger block of land surrounded by sage-bush hills and sustained by a creek of clear spring water that is now home to some 150 hounds and a thriving livery and riding business. We met Lynn sitting at her desk wearing a check waistcoat and a flat cap, looking for all the world like a reincarnation of Ronnie Wallace. We later watched her put the hounds to bed by calling each one individually on to its lodge after feeding, in a manner that was the opposite of normal practice in the UK, where hounds are called into the feed yard before dividing themselves into dog and bitch lodges afterwards. We were told that hounds are sometimes fed in the sprawling grass yard, which is the final resting place for any horse whose time is up. Having shot the horse, Lynn simply opened up the belly with a penknife and let the hounds do the rest. 'There's nothing left', she told us. 'They eat bones, intestines, hide and all.'

Lynn and her younger whipper-in and companion, Angela Murray, brought sixty-seven hounds to the meet the following morning, where three resounding cheers welcomed Grosvenor and me to the hunt, and put the wind up several hounds unused to such a racket. Things did not quite go according to plan to begin with; hounds rioted on a strong bull calf and then gobbled up a large jackrabbit before eventually finding the quarry they were supposed to hunt. It is easy to run out of horse power in this steep and rugged county, and Grosvenor and I were completely outclassed by Lynn during the ensuing long run, which left her alone with hounds and the rest of us hopelessly out of touch. I recalled a similar feeling when hunting with the Cotswold back home after Julian Barnfield and his hounds disappeared amongst the Miserden valleys to make a fine four-mile point. Despite the views of some followers, no huntsman likes to give his field the slip, especially when hounds go on to score a good hunt as the Red Rock did that day.

We had one last appointment to keep before flying home. The Red Rock Hunt Ball in Reno was held in the enormous Silver Legacy hotel; the complex was so big that a Julio Iglesias concert took place somewhere on the premises the same evening without us ever being aware that it was happening. We arrived at the hotel lobby carrying our red coats and still wearing top boots, but no one gave our strange, dusty figures so much as a second glance. After dinner Grosvenor and I announced the Grand Canyon Hunt as winners of the extraordinary competition it had been our privilege to judge, with a special mention for Joe Emile's tough workers at the Knoxville and the only hunt we had seen properly concluded during our visit. My trip to the west had revealed a hard, uncompromising land that is home to some of the most dedicated hound men and women I had ever met and, in the coyote, the toughest quarry imaginable.

The desire to emulate English hunting in far-flung lands is remarkable, even more so where exponents seek to retain customs and traditions that have been left behind on our side of the pond. There is no escaping the fact that the damp, mild climate enjoyed by Great Britain and Ireland makes our green islands uniquely suitable for hunting with hounds; one only has to witness the stamina, activity and enthusiasm of hounds going about their work to understand this. Our sport has also developed and evolved in tandem with the rural landscape and those who live and work amongst the farmland, mountains and moors where hunting has always flourished. It is this unique and natural capacity for British and Irish hunting to involve people from every strata of rural society that sets our hunting apart from that of everywhere else in the world.

CHAPTER 24

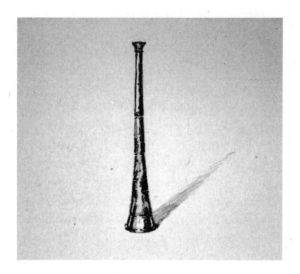

A return to the horn

Hunting journalism had its moments; however, the rewards of writing about other people's hounds and hunting counties were small beer compared with being in the hot seat. I was often asked whether I missed it, and my answer was always the same: I missed the hounds and the hunting beyond measure, but nothing else; hunt balls, committee meetings, fund raisers, country fairs and point-to-points were events to be endured solely for the benefit of the hunt. Walking alongside the tiny Riccal to visit the Bentley family one Christmas Eve, I disturbed a fox sitting tight amongst thistles on the beck side. As he loped away beneath a cold, wintry sky, I yearned for a pack of hounds to clap on to his line, and a high mettled hunter to jump up and ride. Against this backdrop the fortunes of my former Sinnington Hunt had reached a low ebb, and the committee had advertised for new masters to come on board and turn the hunt around. As I lived in the heart of the Sinnington vale, the opportunity to help to restore the fortunes of my former hunt was a challenge that could not be ignored, despite my distaste for the fund raising and socialising this would entail.

I formed a joint mastership with the late Countess's grandson, Fred Collin, who had enjoyed some of our great hunting runs in the 1990s, and a serene and beautiful lady who became my brilliant field master and, later, much cherished wife. The infrastructure of a wild hunting country populated by knowledgeable locals was very much intact; John Cranage was still whipping-in wearing a red coat, and Wilf Gamble could still be relied upon to help out when needed at the kennels. A young boy who had found and then welded back together my lost hunting horn twenty years earlier was now the hunt's trusted and hard working countryman; James Otterburn's friends, Robs Easton and Marsden, had grown up to become gamekeepers keen to welcome and accommodate the hunt. Caroline Scott, whose partner had been one of the outgoing masters, agreed to take on the hunt horses, and Giles Bennett telephoned to ask for the kennel huntsman's position.

My reappointment as master coincided with an invitation to join the committee of the MFHA under the Chairmanship of Stephen Lambert. We met in London three times a year to discuss and ratify a whole raft of issues broadly related to hunting, including the ever-changing political backdrop, hunt amalgamations, point-to-point racing and hound welfare at kennels. The current Chief Executive of the Countryside Alliance, Tim Bonner, was on hand to provide an update of any pending prosecutions and offer advice on hunting within the law. Under the Directorship of Tim Easby, the MFHA are quick to help and update masters on new and current legislation, such as employment, health and safety, and the introduction of compulsory microchipping for hounds. Thanks to this guidance, there is no need for masters to fall foul of the law, and in the case of microchipping, training sessions were organised that allowed hunts to save valuable time and money.

Other key issues under consideration during my time on the committee included the close scrutiny of hunt insurance policies, the role of the association going forward and a possible amendment to the Hunting Act, which would have brought the law into line with that in Scotland where a full pack of hounds can be used to control foxes with guns. Whilst recognising the obvious benefits, I was not entirely comfortable about the consequences of such a move, for I had spent most of my life arguing passionately against the gun as a method of fox control. It was views such as this that led Tim Bonner to describe me as a fundamentalist; I took his point on board but felt it was perhaps a little harsh. After my three-year stint was up, I left the committee having gained a valuable insight into the enormous amount of work that goes into safeguarding our sport, much of it from individuals who give freely of their time.

In December Tom Cranage and I drove down to Kirby Bellars in Leicestershire, where I had tracked down representatives of the cherished Puckeridge Actress line flourishing in the Quorn kennels, but inexplicably lost from the Sinnington pack. Gone also was the treasured tail female line to Old Dominion Gorgeous who had been a gift to the hunt from the late Captain Wallace. Litter sisters Quorn Booty and Bombshell '09 were reunited with my original Border outcross via Zetland Woodcock to produce the finest litter I have ever bred, and hounds that are still cutting out the work today. I inherited some top-class hounds from Tony Winter such as Partner '07, Foxglove '05 and Garland '06 who represented the other old Sinnington line, and benefited from the generosity of Frank Houghton-Brown, Andrew Osborne and Mark Hankinson, who offered drafts from the Tynedale, Bedale and Wilton. Most conspicuous of these was a heavy sixth-season dog with a badger-pie coat, slack jowls and a voice to waken the dead; time and again Tynedale Warrior '06's melodious roar from the darkest depths of a thick thorn covert proclaimed the start of hunt. The Bedale's Holly '09 and Habit '06 were equally low-scenting; the former had a distinctive strangulated voice, the latter only half a stern, whilst Tynedale Rockwood '09 possessed the drive to push on well forward at a check and recover the line.

After an eleven-year break from owning horses, I now had to find some good ones at the right price. Ash Bealby telephoned out of the blue to explain that he had the perfect horse for the job in Alfie, a handsome middle-aged chestnut who went on to carry me well for the next three seasons, while Jessica Harrington generously came up with a hot-blooded eventer that her daughter no longer wished to compete. Paris could take a nice hold and had the infuriating habit of jinking suddenly at full gallop, but he never contemplated turning his head from a fence. Philip Hobbs very kindly sent up a retired steeplechaser that had won a race at the Cheltenham Festival, but was tragically killed out hunting in a collision with another horse. The equine team was completed by a purchase from John and Judi Thurloe: the most expensive horse of the lot, but as it turned out, not the best.

With staff, kennels and stables sorted, it was time to look in closer detail at the country I knew so well. The Countess of Feversham's adage still held true, although the difficult 25 per cent had dug in their heels during the intervening years. A new generation of farmers did not necessarily feel the same away about hunting as had their fathers; some extended a warmer welcome than had previously been the case, but others made it clear that we were not welcome at all. One young lady who now controls land beside a Sinnington Hunt covert wrote a vile and vitriolic letter warning us off her small farm only a week after chatting to me amicably with her young daughter at the hunt Pony Club camp. When we discussed the letter at a masters meeting, Fred came up with the memorable line, 'But I thought it was supposed to be fun'. We later had an unpalatable meeting with the agent representing the leaseholder of Fred's own Bransdale moor, during which we learnt that Fred's decision to join the mastership had not met with universal approval.

The Sinnington country includes several thousand acres of land utilised by the Forestry Commission on very long leases, and a smaller area that is owned by the Commission outright. I asked the relevant landowners for sight of the long leases, which without exception reserved the sporting rights to the owner and his assignees. One lease even went so far as to specifically reserve hunting rights, without distinguishing between the different forms of hunting. Since the Hunting Act became law, hunts were forced to apply for a licence to hunt on Forestry Commission land, but it did not stop there. It was also necessary to explain exactly where trails were to be laid, and to suffer the presence of an official ranger on hunt days, however, far worse was the open availability of this information to the general public. In light of these restrictions I could see little future in trying to progress hunting on government-owned land, but attempted to establish the definition of sporting rights when meeting Forestry Commission officials in Pickering. They were adamant that such rights referred only to shooting and hunting a live quarry, but I could not accept their argument that drag hunting did not qualify. As it happens, we muddled through just fine, but it would have been interesting to test the definition of sporting rights in a court of law, and resolve the ambiguity of hunting on land where the Forestry Commission is not an owner, but a tenant.

There was much to offset these difficulties and disappointments. A previously inaccessible farm surrounded by mains electricity on the Derwent boundary had fallen into friendly hands, and Tim Easterby had expanded his already-large acreage to provide a veritable playground for the hunt, and make Habton the most popular meet in the vale. At Welburn Ings Will Shaw built several hunt jumps across his lovely grass farm, just as his father had done more than twenty years earlier. Rosanna James, whose father Gordon Foster had hunted hounds with distinction between the wars, invited me to join her for a ride around her lovely high side grass farm in Sleightholmedale. I was shown long-forgotten crossing places over the Hodge Beck, hunt jumps designed to be taken fifteen abreast and rides newly cut out and cleared. Much of this work had been done by Colin Short, who had been replaced as head keeper by the new management of Bransdale Moor and was now working as a freelance countryman.

There was no longer a shoot at Nunnington, where the Clive family were as welcoming and helpful as I remembered, and the shoot at Ness had begun to downgrade after several busy years. The larger high side shoots were as receptive to hunting as ever, many of them keepered by men who I first knew as boys. James Holt had surrendered control of his Ravenswick shoot to a supportive tenant, and sold off the big house that had been a Mecca for hospitality and entertainment throughout the 1990s. Rainwater now poured through gaping holes in the roof, and the wind howled through windowless rooms where wine and laughter had once flowed in equal measure. The house endures to this day, standing like a wreck from the blitz, and waiting patiently for the transformation that will surely come. Men such as Keith Preston, Dick Scott and Tange Pickard still turned out regularly to follow hounds by car, although Tange's gate-making days were long gone.

The greatest change was to be seen amongst the mounted field, where several new faces had appeared to replace those, such as Peter Easterby, who were no longer riding to hounds. The farmer and racehorse trainer used to field master for me in the early days and went straight as a die across country. He once invited a neighbouring farmer whose winter corn he had galloped over to help himself to a few laps in the combine of his own wheat fields come harvest. A few of the old-timers were still going strong, including my own dear parents, Robert and Pauline Edwards-Harrison, and Patrick and Bridget Till. Robert and Pauline exemplified the saintly stamp of stalwart hunt supporter who is permanently on standby to roll up sleeves and set to work at any fund-raising event. Bridget Till had served as hunt secretary in the 1990s, and later as a joint master when Richard Mould came back to hunt hounds as a professional. Her husband possessed a unique ability to disarm people with a cutting one-liner, but was a devoted supporter of hunting and a prolific walker of hound puppies.

I had new neighbours too; Sean McClarron had taken on the Derwent while Tom Holt was in his third season at the Middleton. Since I had known Tom throughout his life, I followed his progress carefully and had enjoyed a wonderful day behind his hounds the previous winter. The idea of Tom taking on the four-days-a-week pack had first been suggested to the unsuspecting young man inside Kirkham Hall, where the owner was entertaining several of us to tea after a day's rough shooting at Firby. On the way home I reminded Tom of the sound advice once given to me by Derek Jackson, which I expect he may have recalled when giving up the hounds seven seasons later.

CHAPTER 25

Sinnington second time around

I had forgotten the pleasures of exercising hounds along verdant green lanes frothing with cow parsley and bright summer greenery; to while away hours in this fashion strengthens the bond between huntsman and hounds and is the finest possible way to start the day. We were soon crossing the A170 into the high country every morning, often bicycling back through Pockley village, where residents told me they had not seen hounds on summer exercise for years. I left Yorkshire only once that first summer, to take up an invitation from my former Chairman, James Holt, to fish for salmon on the Beauly. He told me there were two house rules to be obeyed: the first fish landed must be released, and dinner is served promptly at 7.30 p.m. One evening I hooked a fresh bar of silver and returned woefully late to the lodge. James looked up from his pudding and grinned. 'I hope you kept it for your puppy show lunch', he said.

When I hunted hounds for the first time after an eleven-year absence it felt as if the intervening years had simply been washed away. There was not much that was different, strange or unfamiliar about that early September morning; just the inspirational clamour of hounds in full cry though the miscanthus, the ebb and flow of a moving horse and a huntsman's single-minded concentration on the job in hand. The morning smelt of hot horse sweat, damp hounds and autumn stubbles; only the acrid aroma of a broken-up fox was absent from the scene. A familiar routine quickly fell into place as hounds gathered momentum to hunt with increasing confidence and style across the unspoilt vale and wilder hills. In common with every other hunt in the country, we found our own private way through the mess of the illogical Hunting Act whilst utilising as much of our traditional hunting country as possible. Rather than announce my intention to hunt within the law at every meet throughout a long season, I preferred to make this statement at the AGM in October, where it could be recorded in the minutes for posterity. Other precautions included being filmed by our conscientious counter-surveillance officer, Peter Bell, as James Otterburn briefed me on the whereabouts of trails laid at the start of each hunting day.

The hunt Chairman's report at the end of my first season back spoke of a renewed energy and optimism surrounding the hunt, but later that summer Ian Garfitt had to deal with sensitive issues surrounding the break-up of my joint master's marriage, and with my and Rachel's subsequent decision to build a life together. Not for the first time, Ian's patient and diplomatic approach was to stand the hunt in good stead, and at no point did I ever feel my position was in jeopardy. The hunt committee supported the Chairman in doing what he believed was best for the hunt, although one lady who had written to congratulate me warmly on my move to the Quorn thirteen years earlier now wrote to say that she no longer wished to indulge the joint master's passion by raising funds for the hunt, which was grossly hypocritical considering her own past conduct. Another resigned as hunt campaigner, although I was not aware that she had ever given the position more than a moment's thought. One landowner spelt out stricter conditions for hunting on his land and made it clear that neither Rachel nor I would ever be welcome in his home again. He has remained true to his word, although I could not begin to count the numerous occasions I crossed the threshold of his house in sunnier times. Genuine Ryedale farmers had very little to say about my new domestic circumstances and chose not to stand in moral judgement; for them it was business as usual. Many others wrote in support, insisting that personal lives had nothing to do with the master's ability to organise a hunting country, although Fred decided that he no longer wished to be part of our team.

Any lingering unpleasantness evaporated once we began hunting again at

Muscoates Whin in early September with Nick Thornicroft as my new kennel huntsman. Giles had been persuaded to join the Holderness on 1 May, where he was no doubt happy to resume looking after old English hounds following his brief interlude with the Sinnington. Young, keen and headstrong, Nick was not one to turn his back on a challenge; during our second Opening Meet he followed me in an attempt to swim the Costa Beck that resulted in us both going for a cold swim. On another occasion he quickly and quietly overpowered a particularly unpleasant agitator who was attempting to bar access to a public bridleway.

My second winter back was one of the wettest on record, but we did not miss a single day and only took to our feet when snow made it impossible for horses. On one occasion hounds ran clean away from us across a waterlogged vale; when we caught up with them near Butterwick, old Warrior was shaking the water from his flanks, having swum the Rye in heavy spate. He was joined by Middleton Punter '07 and a promising second season dog named Merlin '11, who was lucky to survive the following year when falling terribly ill after a day on the high side. The vet was able to save his life in a costly operation that was generously paid for by Benoit Guerin, and has since established himself as a hound of exceptional ability. We had a brilliant high side day from the Becketts' Rievaulx meet in early February when hounds ran in and out of steep, limestone ravines, before settling into the rhythm of a fine two-and-a-half hour afternoon hunt that was frequently redeemed by Bedale Holly '09 at her low-scenting best. There was something about the demeanour of the hounds as they came back in dribs and drabs from the morning run that made me return the next day. No pot of gold at a rainbow's end could have matched my discovery of the well-worried corpse of an enormous dog fox. Although hounds must have changed on to his line, they were only performing a task their ancestors had done for centuries before them, and I felt no inclination to report this hiccup to officers of the state.

I found myself asking the Mother Superior of a nunnery near Wass for permission to retrieve hounds in similar circumstances a month later, which she quickly and happily granted. The high side came up trumps again following the last-ever meet at Wytherstone House, with two fast and long hunts through Riccal Dale, Goodhams Dale and Skiplam. After our season in Yorkshire had ended, the VWH joint master, Julian Weston, invited our hounds down to Gloucestershire for a memorable day's hunting in the sprawling but well ridden woodlands of Cirencester Park. Sidney Bailey was on hand to see the Sinnington hounds at their absolute best as fourteen-and-a-half couple ran with relentless determination until nightfall, completely ignoring fallow deer, roe and muntjac that criss-crossed the line throughout the day. Looking back, it is hard to recall a day's hunting I have enjoyed more than that very special visit to a landscape I had known and loved since Cirencester days.

During my third season back at the Sinnington I began to resent the many compromises thrust upon me by the Hunting Act, and the blind faith required to properly nurture a hunting country. I had always treasured the unassailable permanence of hunting, the careful breeding of hounds, the long-term management of coverts and the encouragement of the next generation. The foundations on which to build these ambitions had become increasingly unstable, and hunting too vulnerable to risks and threats over which I had no control. With the hounds going well and the hunt in good shape, the time had come to hand over the ruling master's silver hunting horn to a younger and different generation. Rachel and I tendered our resignations after an especially good day from the Harome end of the vale in early January, but I have seldom felt more certain of doing the right thing. The Chairman and committee were not quite as supportive over our resignation as I had hoped; perhaps they felt five years would have been better than three, but my mind was made up.

There were several applicants for the position of master, including one from my kennel huntsman. After little deliberation, we appointed Tom Roberts to take over as sole master on 1 May, for he possessed the confidence, passion and wherewithal necessary for the job. I hope that Tom would agree that he inherited a useful pack of hounds and an open country in good heart. Less than three months into his first season my former pack produced a superb seven-mile point across the vale. I was thrilled. My job was done.

CHAPTER 26

The future

As I had discovered, nostalgia in hunting is not particularly healthy; a huntsman is better served looking forwards rather than back. But with every passing season the number of huntsmen who plied their trade before the ban diminishes. There could come a time when none are left, in which case the future of our sport would lie in the hands of those who have only ever hunted hounds since the ban came into force. We all hope for repeal but, as the years roll on, such a lifeline to hunting seems increasingly remote. There was renewed hope for a beneficial amendment to the Act in 2015, but that was dashed when Nicola Sturgeon and her Scottish Members of Parliament reneged on a pledge not to vote on English matters of law. The next generation of huntsmen may not have carried the horn before the ban became law, but many grew up knowing and understanding the pre-ban ways. The responsibility for ensuring that the correct protocols for handling hounds in the hunting field are passed on to successive generations is in their hands. Once lost, those ways may never be recovered.

The age-old dichotomy between moving with the times and retaining old traditions represents one of hunting's greatest challenges: which practices to discard, which to retain and which to introduce. I cannot be the only one flinching when certain social media images of hunting flicker across a screen. We see photographs of hedges that are guaranteed to be jumped on the morrow, endless footage of horses galloping and jumping without sight or sound of hounds, even pictures of riders clambering all over their horses like clowns. I hope such neglect of the fundamental role played by the foxhound in our sport is not the beginning of the end for a breed treasured for its many and remarkable attributes, for I have seen at first-hand the consequences of breeding hounds purely to pursue a drag. It has been the consistent importance attached by hound breeders to virtues such as voice, stamina, nose and fox sense over the last three hundred years that has produced the superlative hunting animal that is the modern foxhound. It would be good to see more images on social media of hounds in full cry, and less footage of riders jumping endless fences without a hound in sight or earshot.

Closer to home, time-honoured events in the sporting year such as the Sinnington Hunt point-to-point are sold to the general public as Helmsley Horse Races, which hardly squares with an MFHA recommendation that hounds should be paraded at hunt race meetings to heighten public awareness of the close connection between two great sports. It sometimes feels as if the PR machine that won hunting so many new friends in the run-up to the ban is now running out of steam, although initiatives such as James Barclay's This is Hunting UK are doing their best to counteract the decline. The way forward is not to keep our heads below the parapet as in the post-war years, but to continue promoting the benefits that hunting brings to both conservation and the wider rural community. In the run-up to the ban, these messages were frequently and skilfully communicated by the Countryside Alliance and the MFHA to such good effect that the media became our ally and not our foe.

If moving with the times represents one of the great challenges to our sport, so a shortage of hunting country represents another. This may not always be a consequence of main roads, development or the dreaded HS2 railway line. It is often to do with increased pressure on whatever green countryside remains. On 14 March during my last season at the Sinnington, I attended the final meet of the Farndale Hunt, whose country had been hunted by hounds ever since the Duke of Buckingham rode those high, wild moors in the late seventeenth century. The Farndale were not compelled to disband due to a lack of country, for they hunted one of the least-populated and remote areas of England, but for no other reason than the impossible pressures of operating in a heavily shot country. Whilst some moorland grouse shoots continued to welcome hounds, others restricted access, refused to lift snares on hunt days and ignored the plight of their local hunt to such an extent that the Farndale had no option but to close down. Their final meet was attended by the largest mounted field for years and more than two hundred supporters on foot; however, the farcical outcome on that fine spring morning was that the Farndale had nowhere to hunt at all, for when a few unkempt saboteurs appeared the shooting tenant forbade access to the dale from which the hunt takes its name. There was stunned disbelief as the sorry news permeated the large crowd of supporters, and hounds were loaded back into their trailers without having left the meet.

Shooting's surge in popularity has been a phenomenon of the last twenty years, and the importance of cultivating a good relationship with shoots cannot be overstated, for the threat posed by shooting to hunting has been whispered many times over the last twenty years. Masters should liaise with shoots at every level. Gamekeepers, shoot tenants and landowners must be offered the genuine hand of friendship and tactfully prevailed upon whenever possible to support their local hunt. That means allowing access on agreed days throughout the season, and not just after shooting has ended in February. If every shoot in the land refused to welcome hounds between November and January, hunting would surely perish; thankfully, there are many shoots willing to help during these sensitive months, but other shoots choose to ignore the plight of their fellow countrymen and women. In return, hunts must do their utmost to honour any undertakings they have given, but should avoid making a rod for their own back by agreeing to the impossible. More hunting and shooting fallouts are attributed to broken promises than anything else; if it cannot be done, don't say it can. It helps enormously if the hunt negotiator is a country person with an understanding of and respect for the other man's sport, for he will appreciate the importance of matters such as avoiding cover crops and allowing birds time to go up to roost. There must be a huge investment of time and energy, combined with understanding and cooperation from both sides, if the Farndale's sorry plight is not to be repeated elsewhere.

Given the pressures and difficulties involved, it is remarkable that there appears to be no shortage of men and women prepared to devote large chunks of their life to becoming an MFH, even more so for those blessed few, amateurs and professionals alike, who aspire to carry the horn. They may sometimes feel the weight of the world upon their shoulders, but they will also have sipped from the draught of heaven. On giving up the horn, I pondered just what I had found quite so compelling about hunting a pack of foxhounds, and decided it was this: it is the electrifying peal of music as the first hound opens, and the relief of a line well found. It is tension easing as hounds settle to their task, followed by carefree minutes suspended in time as they rattle joyously around covert. There is not much that can go wrong at this stage, but everything changes with a spine-tingling 'holloa' to signal the next phase of the hunt. A moment of anxiety and excitement in equal measure; the fear of a run squandered before it has properly begun, combined with the excitement and glorious uncertainty of where it might end. If hounds falter at this crucial moment, the huntsman must decide whether to risk concentration by blowing them on to the line, or allow them hour-long seconds of silence.

Everything is at stake during the next ten or fifteen minutes. A bad check, the interference of riot, electric fencing to hurt and confuse, and a great deal more can so easily conspire to turn a promising hunt into a muddled and frustrating pursuit with no future. If hounds survive such hindrances for a mile or more, the whole pack comes together as one, growing in confidence, cry and momentum as they settle true to the line. On rare occasions this happy state is evident from the very start of a hunt; sometimes it can take half an hour or more. Occasionally it does not arrive at all. This glorious fusion is a moment of truth that separates the tenuous and vulnerable from the confident and unassailable. And for the huntsman, a growing euphoria inspired by a deep love and pride for the hounds ahead.

The longer the pack is able to hunt without interference, the greater the likelihood of hounds resolving a check unassisted. Although a successful cast to recover the line is always gratifying, a huntsman's greater pleasure is for hounds to manage it alone. I love the story of how two young subalterns were overheard discussing the merits of Sir Peter Farquhar after a fabulous day behind his bitches in the Portman vale. 'Brilliant day', said one, 'but I don't think much of the huntsman. He never said a word'. There is, of course, the additional thrill of crossing country on a good horse during a fast run; the split-second decision of where to jump in and out of each field, the anticipation of the hunt's direction and the powerful surge of a brave horse that never turns its head from a fence, no matter how formidable it is. At some indefinable stage of the hunt, the reality of a successful conclusion becomes apparent, and when that is achieved there comes an unsurpassed sensation of elation, and gratitude for hounds that have given their all. Simply put, there is no better feeling in the world.

Index

Thornton, John (Nat) 22,
23, 33–4
Thornton, Martin 82, 119,
139
thoroughbred yearling sales,
USA 31
Thorpe Trussels covert 89
threats, hunt protesters
109, 113, 114, 125.
see also house attack
three-day week, Quorn
Hunt 119–20, 125
'The Thrush' (nickname) 50
Thurloe, John and Judi
167
Thurlow Hunt 147
Till, Bridget 74, 169
Till, Patrick 65, 68, 74,
169
Tilton Hills, Leicestershire
105, 115, 116, 121
Tindall, Joe 145
Tiverton Staghounds 153
To the Manor Born TV
show 132
Today programme,
Radio 4 77
Todd, Stephen 60–1, 78
Todenham Manor 22
Todhunter, Barry 82, 155
Tomlinson, Luke 107
Tomlinson, Simon 143
Townsend, Joe 146
Toye, Frank 34
tradition 97, 101, 120,
148, 149, 175–6. see also
rural way of life
traffic. see road traffic/road
networks
travel company, Wild and
Exotic 141–2
Trinidad, overseas hunting

157–8
Trotter, Diana 30
Turner, Christopher 26
Turner, George 41–2
Two Bridges Hunt Club
meet, Dartmoor 45
Twyford Brook,
Leicestershire 110
Tyacke, Richard, Penny
and Richard (Junior) 72,
146, 155

Uloth, Rupert 121
Upper Broughton,
Leicestershire 97,
109–10, 118
urbanisation 111, 118, 119
USA, overseas hunting 31,
137, 159–60

Vale of White Horse
(VWH) Hunt 130,
132–3, 143–4, 152
Vestey, Edmund 147
Vickers, Rodney 116
video, Quorn 90, 103
Voorspuy, Tristan 114
murder of 158–9
VWH. see Vale of White
Horse (VWH) Hunt

Wade, Bouskell 89
Waggie the horse 42, 48,
50, 55, 69, 99–100, 110,
111
Wakeham, Willie 83, 87,
115
Wales and Border Counties
Hounds Show 131–2
Walker strain of hound
163
Walkham Valley, Dartmoor

38
Wallace, Captain Ronnie
66, 87, 90, 120, 132,
135, 145, 154, 163, 167
grave of 146
Wallace, David 87
Walton Thorns,
Leicestershire 92, 119
Ward, Mick 95
Wardle, Tot 48–9
Warren's Gorse meet,
Beaufort Hunt 156
Wartnaby estate,
Leicestershire 93–5, 100,
105
Warwickshire Hunt 130,
147
water supply, Spooners and
West Dartmoor Hunt 34
Watts, Charlie 115
Waugh, Adam 131
Welbeck estate,
Nottinghamshire 147
Welburn Manor, North
Yorkshire 49–50
Wellfield Plantation,
Cirencester Park 143–4
Westbury, Lord 59
Western Hunt Challenge,
USA 159–64
West of England Hound
Show, Honiton 132
Weston, Julian 173
Wharton, Terry 72
Whatoff Farm meet,
Quorn Hunt 91, 111
Wheeler, Charles 48
White-Spunner, General
Sir Barney 73, 108
Wild and Exotic travel
company 141–2
wildlife 55, 75–9

Adrian Dangar became MFH and huntsman of the Spooners & West Dartmoor Hunt at the age of 24 and never looked back. MFH to the Sinnington in North Yorkshire (twice) and only the second amateur huntsman in 300 years to be appointed MFH to the Quorn in Leicestershire. As a writer he contributes on a regular basis to Country Life, The Field, Horse & Hound and Trout & Salmon, has judged all the major hound shows in Britain, including the Peterborough Royal Foxhound Show three times, the Australian hound show twice, and the Western Hunt Challenge in the USA. He is the founding owner and Managing Director of Wild and Exotic, a company specialising in riding safaris and tailor made travel around the world. His favourite pastimes are hunting, the pursuit of woodcock and chasing salmon in remote streams on the west coast of Scotland.